P9-CQF-087

Be Anxious for Nothing
Study Guide

by
Joyce Meyer

Warner Faith

WARNER BOOKS

An AOL Time Warner Company

If you purchase this book without a cover you should be aware that this book may have been stolen property and reported as "unsold and destroyed" to the publisher. In such case neither the author nor the publisher has received any payment for this "stripped book."

Unless otherwise indicated, all Scriptures quotations are taken from *The Amplified Bible* (AMP). *The Amplified Bible, Old Testament* copyright © 1965, 1987 by The Zondervan Corporation. *The Amplified New Testament,* copyright © 1954, 1958, 1987 by the Lockman Foundation. Used by permission.

Scripture quotations marked "KJV" are taken from the *King James Version* of the Bible.

Scripture quotations marked "NIV" are taken from the *Holy Bible, New International Version*®. NIV®. Copyright 1973, 1978, 1984 by International Bible Society. Used by permission of Zondervan Publishing House. All rights reserved.

Scripture quotations marked "NASB" are taken from the *New American Standard Bible*®, © copyright The Lockman Foundation 1960, 1962, 1963, 1968, 1971, 1972, 1973, 1975, 1977. Used by permission.

Scripture quotations marked "WORRELL" are taken from *The Worrell New Testament* © 1904 by A.S. Worrell. Copyright assigned to the Assemblies of God, Springfield, MO. Edition published in 1980 by the Gospel Publishing House, Springfield, MO 65802.

Direct quotations from Scripture are enclosed in quotation marks.

WARNER BOOKS EDITION

Copyright © 2002 by Joyce Meyer
Life In The Word, Inc.
P.O. Box 655
Fenton, Missouri 63026
All rights reserved.

Warner Books, Inc., 1271 Avenue of the Americas, New York, NY 10020

Visit our Website at www.twbookmark.com.

An AOL Time Warner Company

Printed in the United States of America
First Warner Faith Printing: October 2002
10 9 8 7 6 5 4 3 2 1

ISBN: 0-446-69105-4
LCCN: 2002110913

Contents

Introduction

*P*eace is available to all who believe in Jesus Christ. It is part of God's plan for our lives through His Son Jesus to be marked by a profound sense of inner peace and serenity. Regardless of our outward circumstances, we are to be enjoying the abundant, joyful, peaceful life that God has intended for us from the beginning. But very few people enjoy this peace as part of the normal condition of their lives.

Many of us have not learned how to entrust ourselves to God and retire from self-care. Like many people in the world, we respond to negative circumstances with restlessness, fear, and apprehension instead of choosing to draw on the peace of God. There are many serious things going on in this world, and we need to be aware of them and prepared for them. But at the same time, we need to learn to relax and take things as they come without getting all nervous and upset about them. God's way is for us to respond with peaceful trust, even when we can't see the way out.

In times of trials, disappointments, and negative circumstances, do you choose trust or torment, anxiety or peace, worry or joy?

I went through a time in my life when I was plagued by worry and anxiety. I lived in a state of turmoil for so many years, I didn't realize how abnormal it really was. In those days I tormented myself with needless worry and apprehension, because I tried to handle everything myself. While I was always a responsible person who took on the responsibility for my life, I also took on the care of it. Once I came to understand 1 Peter 5:7 that says we are to cast our care upon the Lord because He cares for us, I started to apply that principle in my life, and I began to truly enjoy it.

You can be free from anxiety and have a happy, joyful life!

As you work through this study guide, you will learn how to replace the stress, frustration, and worry in your life with victory and peace. I believe that this new knowledge will help you enter the rest of God by taking what the devil tries to give you, turning it over to the Lord, and watching Him turn it into good in accordance with His perfect will and plan for you.[1]

USING THIS STUDY GUIDE

The purpose of this workbook is to reinforce the principles taught in my book, *Be Anxious for Nothing*. You will need a copy of *Be Anxious for Nothing* to work through this book.

This study guide is written in a question and answer format. By reading a chapter in *Be Anxious for Nothing*, studying the designated Scripture verses, and answering the questions in the corresponding chapter of the study guide, you will gain a deeper understanding of the principles and learn more easily how to incorporate them into your daily life.

To use this workbook, look up and read the corresponding chapter in *Be Anxious for Nothing*. Next look up in your Bible the Scriptures designated in the study guide and read them. This is an important step because those Scriptures are the basis of the teaching in that particular chapter and are taken directly from that chapter.

Answer the questions in the study guide by referring to the appropriate chapter in *Be Anxious for Nothing*. Once you have finished answering the questions in each chapter, turn to the answer key in the back of this book to check your answers.

1. Work at a comfortable pace. Don't rush to finish quickly. Stay in each chapter until you have a thorough understanding of the material and how it pertains to your life.

2. Follow these steps with each chapter in this study guide.

3. Use this study guide for individual study or group discussion. When using it in a group, discuss your answers and learn how to apply the principles in a way that may not have occurred to you until you heard the experiences of others.

Consistently and steadily working through this book will empower you to gradually improve the way you respond to difficult times and receive by faith what God desires you to have — His help. Choosing to live in peace and joy rather than to be burdened with worry and anxiety will enable you to change things in your life that you thought you would have to live with forever.

LIVE IN PEACE

Anxiety steals your joy and peace and torments and hinders you from enjoying your life according to God's plan. How happy, joyful and peaceful are you? If you have a problem in this area, I believe the God-directed, God-empowered principles in this guidebook are important tools that will help you to start giving God all your worry, concern, anxiety, and care — and start living in peace as a normal condition.

It is my sincere prayer that working through this study guide, along with the book, *Be Anxious for Nothing,* will help firmly establish in your heart forever that no matter what happens, as you trust God, you will have the privilege of being cared for by the One Who knows and does all things well. When you are secure in that knowledge, you will enjoy a life filled with God's best for you.

1. Read Philippians 4:6,7 NASB; 1 Peter 5:6,7 NASB

    a. As believers in Jesus Christ, what is to be the normal condition for us? _____.

    b. In His Word, what does God tell us to do? _____

    _____

    _____.

    c. Many people are familiar with these Scriptures but _____

    _____ what these Scriptures instruct.

    d. Sometimes we are so accustomed to responding in a natural way to the circumstances we experience in life as unbelievers around us do, how do we spend much of our time?_____

    _____

    _____

    _____.

    e. Instead, what could we be doing? _____

    _____!

    f. In the author's own case, when did she begin to experience the peace of God? _____

    _____

    _____.

    g. If you are not living in the peace of God, you can _____

    _____.

PART 1

Be Anxious for Nothing

Jesus and Peace

*I*n the original book, *Be Anxious for Nothing,* read Chapter 1, then read in your Bible the Scriptures designated below and answer the questions that follow. When you finish, check your answers in the answer key provided at the end of this book.

As you continue to follow this procedure throughout this workbook, you can be assured that you will gain insight through understanding that will help you integrate these godly principles into your daily life and be free from anxiety!

1. Read John 14:27; Psalm 91; John 10:10; Ephesians 3:20; 2 Chronicles 16:9; Isaiah 9:6; John 16:33; 14:1; Romans 14:17; Luke 17:21; 2 Corinthians 5:21; Galatians 5:22,23

    a. Jesus' statement in John 14:27 is worded as though He _____ _____ us His peace.

    b. What does it mean that Jesus left us His peace? _____ _____ _____ _____.

    c. What does the Bible show us about the peace Jesus left us? _____.

    d. What does Psalm 91 reveal to us about God's protection? __ _____ _____ _____.

e. Based on John 10:10, Ephesians 3:20, and 2 Chronicles 16:9, what does God want to do for us? Why? _____

_____

_____

_____

_____

_____ .

f. As Christians, our salvation guarantees us a trouble-free life. True or false? _____ .

g. We will still encounter problems. Every one of us at different times in our life go through seasons when things don't work out the way we would like. In John 16:33, what does Jesus, the Prince of Peace, tell us regarding this? _____

_____

_____

_____ .

h. In John 14:1 and 27, just before His return to His Father in heaven, what words did Jesus leave us about our hearts? ____

_____

_____ .

i. Romans 14:17 tells us that Kingdom living is _____

_____

_____ .

j. According to Luke 17:21, where is the Kingdom of God? __

_____ .

k. When were we made righteous, or made in rightstanding with God? _____

_____.

l. What are two of the fruit of the Holy Spirit that are inside those of us who believe in Jesus? _____

_____.

m. How do we enter into the joy and peace of God's kingdom?

_____.

2. Read Romans 15:13; Hebrews 4:9-11; Mark 10:15; Luke 10:20; Habakkuk 3:18 KJV; Psalm 16:11; 1 John 4:12-15; John 14:23

a. With what does the passage in Romans 15:13 tell us that God will fill us? Why? _____

_____

_____

_____

_____.

b. According to the writer of Hebrews, who may enter into the blessed Sabbath rest of the Lord? _____

_____.

c. What is required to enter this rest?_____

_____.

d. Why have members of the church sometimes lost the joy of their salvation? _____

_____.

e. In Luke 10:20, Jesus tells us we should rejoice, not because we have power over the demons or circumstances of this life, but because _____

_____.

f. As believers, our joy and peace are not based in doing and achieving, but in _____.

g. Based on Psalm 16:11, 1 John 4:12-15 and John 14:23, how then do joy and peace come? Why? _____

_____

_____

_____

_____

_____

_____.

h. Where do we experience peace? _____

_____

_____

_____.

i. To summarize this section, joy and peace come from _____

_____

_____.

It's OK to Lighten Up!

Chapter

2

As with the previous chapter, before answering the questions below, first read the corresponding chapter in *Be Anxious for Nothing,* then the Scriptures designated below. After you complete the chapter, check the answer key in the back of this book.

To gain the greatest benefit from this workbook, continue using this method throughout.

1. Read Proverbs 12:25

    a. The Bible teaches that anxiety brings _____ _____ to a person's life.

    b. How does the dictionary define *anxiety?* _____ _____ _____ _____.

    c. Are you ever bothered by this kind of anxiety without knowing what it is? _____.

2. Read Proverbs 15:15; Song of Solomon 2:15 KJV; review John 14:1,27; 16:33; read Mark 4:17

    a. Based on Proverbs 15:15, the author says that once when she went through a period in her life when she was plagued by anxiety, fear, and dread, the Lord told her what was troubling her. What was it? _____ _____.

b. What does Song of Solomon 2:15 KJV call the things we become upset over that are just not worth becoming upset over? _____

_____ .

c. If our life consists of becoming upset over one little thing that really doesn't matter after another, what will be the result?

_____

_____ .

d. In other words, what was Jesus saying to us in John 14:1 and 27 about letting our hearts be troubled and afraid?_____

_____ .

e. What can we see from John 14:27?_____

_____

_____

_____

_____

_____

_____ .

f. Based on Mark 4:17, why will we have persecution? _____

_____ .

g. In today's language, what was Jesus' answer for the tribulation we all experience in our daily lives? _____ .

h. What gives us plenty of reason to calm down and cheer up?

_____

_____ .

    i. If you experience anxiety as a result of deep hurts from the past, although it is not always easy, how can you become free from that emotional bondage?_____ _____!

3.   Read 1 Peter 3:4

    a. According to Peter, what kind of spirit does God like?_____ _____ _____.

    b. What does it mean to be "wrought up"? _____ _____.

    c. What does it mean to be "anxious"?_____ _____ _____.

    d. Why does the devil try to make us tense, get us tied up in knots, upset, disturbed, worried, disquieted, and distracted?

_____

_____

_____

_____

_____.

    e. Based on the author's past experience, if we are so tense, worried, and wrought up we blow everything way out of proportion, what do we need to learn to do? _____

_____

_____

_____

_____

_____.

4. Read Psalm 118:24 KJV; 1 Peter 5:8; review John 10:10

    a. What else does *anxiety* mean? _____

    _____

    _____

    _____

    _____.

    b. The author says that the Lord once told her what causes anxiety. What is the cause? _____

    _____

    _____

    _____

    _____

    _____

    _____

    _____.

    c. Even though we are to learn to lighten up and enjoy life, what are we also told to do in 1 Peter 5:8? _____

    _____

    _____

    _____

    _____.

    d. Based on John 10:10, what do we need to learn to do?_____

    _____

_____
_____.

e. In spite of all the troubling things going on around us in the world, according to the author, what should be our daily confession? _____

_____
_____.

f. What else do we Christians need to do more of? What would happen if we did so? _____

_____
_____.

g. It is easy to find plenty to worry about. To be happy, we need to _____

_____.

5. Read Philippians 4:4,6,7; 2 Corinthians 3:18; review Psalm 16:11

a. Twice in Philippians 4:6,7 what does the apostle Paul tell us to do? What else does he urge us to do? _____

_____
_____
_____
_____.

b. What is one way we develop spiritual maturity? _____

_____
_____.

c. What does Paul mean when he tells us in 2 Corinthians 3:18 that we are constantly being transformed into the image of God and that we are going "from one degree of glory to another"?_____

_____

_____.

d. What do we then need to learn? _____

_____

_____.

e. Instead of postponing being glad until everything is perfect, what do we need to do? _____

_____

_____

_____.

f. According to the author, the doorway to happiness is expressed in the words of the song to the Lord that says,

_____

_____.

g. Based on Psalm 16:11, the fullness of joy is found in God's

_____ — not in His

_____!

h. True joy comes from seeking God's _____.

i. To live in the fullness of the joy of the Lord, what must we do? _____.

  j. Why will we always have opportunities to be anxious, worried, and fretful? _____

_____

_____

_____.

  k. When the devil tries to bring anxiety into our heart, what must we do? Why?_____

_____

_____

_____

_____

_____

_____.

6. Read Psalm 34:19

  a. Although there are many evils that confront us, how many main categories of anxiety are there?_____.

  b. What are they? _____

_____

_____

_____.

7. Read Ecclesiastes 5:1; 2 Corinthians 6:2; Hebrews 3:7,15; 4:7-9; John 8:58; Matthew 6:25-34; 1 Peter 5:7

  a. What is the author's personal definition of anxiety? _____

_____

_____.

b. What was the Lord referring to in the Bible when He said, "Today is the day of salvation," when He said that today if we will hear His voice, that today if we will believe, we will enter into His rest? _____

_____.

c. Instead of spending our time in the past or the future, what do we need to do? _____

_____

_____.

d. Why do we find it so hard to give ourselves to one thing at a time? _____

_____

_____

_____.

e. What does the Bible mean when it tells us in Ecclesiastes 5:1 to give our mind to what we are doing, to "keep our foot" — our footing? _____

_____.

f. There is an anointing on_____.

g. Based on what Jesus said in John 8:58, why do we, as His disciples, find life hard for us if we try to live in the past or the future?_____

_____.

h. In Matthew 6:25-34 Jesus plainly told us that _____

_____

_____

_____

_____

_____

_____.

    i.   Why don't we need to be concerned about tomorrow? _____

        _____

        _____.

    j.   What should we do instead? _____

        _____.

    k.   Why do we need to stop wasting our precious "now"? _____

        _____.

    l.   According to 1 Peter 5:7, we are to _____
        our responsibility, but we are to _____
        our care? Why? _____

        _____.

    m. We are to _____ from the past and
        _____ for the future,
        but we are to _____ in the present.

8.   Read Mark 13:11,9; Romans 8:28

    a. In the passage in Mark 13:11, Jesus was warning His disciples
       that _____

       _____

       _____

       _____.

b. How did He finish His remarks? Why? _____

_____

_____

_____

_____

_____

_____ .

c. If you are filled with anxiety before a conversation, it may be a sign that _____

_____

_____

_____ .

d. Of course, we need to be prepared, but if we excessively rehearse a conversation over and over, it is an indication

_____

_____ .

e. In that case, what will be the result? _____

_____

_____ !

f. We need to ask the Lord to give us_____ with all those to whom we speak. Why? _____

_____

_____

_____

_____

_____ .

9.   Read Luke 10:38-42

    a.   In this passage, what difference do we see between one sister, Martha, and the other sister, Mary? _____

        _____

        _____

        _____

        _____

        _____.

    b.   What did the Lord once tell the author about herself? _____

        _____

        _____.

    c.   What did she need to learn? _____

        _____

        _____

        _____

        _____

        _____!

    d.   Is this a lesson you need to learn also? Why or why not?

        _____

        _____

        _____.

1.   Read Jeremiah 17:5; John 3:6

  a.   What two vastly different arms does the Bible speak of? ___
     _____ .

  b.   How do they differ? Explain._____
     _____
     _____
     _____
     _____
     _____
     _____
     _____
     _____ .

  c.   Based on John 3:6, what is begun in the flesh must be
     _____ in the flesh, but what
     is begun in the Spirit is _____
     by the Spirit.

  d.   What is the difference between trying to operate in the arm of
     the flesh and operating in the arm of the Lord? _____
     _____
     _____
     _____
     _____ .

  e.   What is the difference between carrying out our own plans
     and schemes and allowing God to start something? _____

_____

_____

_____

_____

_____.

f. Many times when we face struggles, we assume the devil is causing us problems, so we try to rebuke him, but that does not always work. Explain. _____

_____

_____

_____

_____.

g. No amount of rebuking the devil will do any good when we are _____

_____.

h. If the work was begun by the Lord, how will it get finished?

_____.

2. Read 1 Corinthians 16:9; 1 John 4:4; Deuteronomy 28:7; James 4:7

a. Whenever we do anything for God, what will happen? ____

_____.

b. Based on 1 John 4:4, what do we need to remember when that happens? _____

_____.

c. According to Deuteronomy 28:7, if we are operating in obe-dience to God's will and plan, what will happen to the enemy? _____
_____.

d. We should not have to spend our lives struggling against the devil. What happens sometimes when we do?_____
_____
_____.

e. In His earthly ministry, why did Jesus not spend a great deal of time fighting against local demons? _____
_____
_____.

f. When we minister in Jesus' name, we have the same power and authority He had. Instead of wearing ourselves out trying to fight spiritual enemies, we should _____
_____
_____.

g. What is the best way to overcome the devil and his demons?
_____
_____
_____.

h. What mistake do many people make in trying to resist the devil?_____
_____!

i. Referring to Christians, what is the difference between a mature individual and immature people?_____

_____

_____

_____

_____

_____.

j. What did the author say happened when she tried to do things her way and in her own power and got out ahead of God? _____

_____.

3. Read Genesis 16:1,2; 15:1-5; 16:3; 17:1-6,15-19; 21:1-14

a. In Genesis 15:1-5, what did the Lord promise Abraham? ____

_____

_____

_____

_____.

b. In Genesis 16:1,2, what plan did Sarah come up with? ____

_____

_____

_____.

c. In Genesis chapter 17, what did the Lord again promise when He appeared to Abraham? _____

_____

_____

_____

_____.

d. Through whom was God's covenant of blessings to be ful-filled? Why? _____

_____

_____

_____

_____

_____

_____.

e. What happened when Isaac was finally born? _____

_____

_____

_____.

f. Many times the reason we are having problems is_____

_____

_____

_____

_____

_____.

g. In such cases, what often happens when things don't turn out the way we expect? _____

_____

_____.

h. When that happens, what do we often fail to remember?___

_____

_____

_____.

4. Read John 6:63; Romans 7:18,24; Proverbs 21:2

    a. In John 6:63, what did Jesus tell us about the Spirit and the flesh? Why? _____

        _____

        _____

        _____.

    b. If we are to fulfill God's will and plan for us in this life, what has to happen? _____

        _____

        _____.

    c. It is from _____

        that the energy of the soul comes forth to cause us all kinds

        of problems on_____.

    d. According to Romans 7:18, Paul had the same problem we have in this area. In that passage, how did he describe himself? _____

        _____

        _____

        _____

        _____.

    e. In verse 24 of that passage, what did Paul end up crying out in his misery and frustration? _____

        _____

        _____

_____
_____
_____.

f. When it seems as though no matter how hard we try to make things work, everything that can go wrong does go wrong, what must we remember? _____

_____
_____.

g. What is the purpose of the testing ground? _____

_____
_____
_____
_____.

h. How can we succeed despite our adversaries and their devices? _____

_____.

i. What is our problem in this area?_____

_____
_____
_____
_____.

j. What often happens to us if God does not bless our plan? ____

_____
_____
_____.

k. Why are there many frustrated, depressed people in our world who have basically given up on God? Are you one of them?_____

_____.

l. When we plan a work of the flesh, as is often the case, what are we trying to do? _____

_____.

m. What should we do instead? _____

_____

_____

_____

_____.

n. As Christians, we all have a work to do. What is it?_____

_____

_____

_____.

o. If God is not in our work, it will be frustrating and depressing. To avoid that, we must learn to discern between what God is truly_____us to do and what we are _____to do.

p. What great revelation does Proverbs 21:2 give us?_____

_____

_____.

q. What mistake do we make that was also made by the Galatians in Paul's day? _____

_____.

5. Read Galatians 4:22-26; 3:1-7; review Romans 15:13

a. The Bible speaks of two covenants. We know them as the old covenant and the new covenant. What else can they be called? _____

_____.

b. On what is the first covenant based? _____

_____

_____

_____.

c. What is the result of that kind of covenant? _____

_____.

d. On what is the second covenant based? _____

_____

_____.

e. What is the result of that kind of covenant? _____

_____.

f. What does each of these covenants bring? _____

_____.

g. Under the first covenant, we _____ we have to do it all; under the second covenant all we have to do is _____, and as part of our believing lifestyle, _____

_____.

h. What is the result of people trying to live by works rather than by God's grace?_____

_____.

i. According to the Word of God, if we will operate in simple, childlike faith, we will _____

_____

_____

_____.

6. Read Galatians 4:27; Isaiah 54:1; review Hebrews 4:10

a. What is the basic message of both Galatians 4:27 and its cross reference, Isaiah 54:1? _____

_____

_____

_____

_____

_____

_____.

b. Why is the Church not seeing the results we want today? __

_____

_____

_____.

c. Based on Galatians 4:27 and Isaiah 54:1, why should a barren woman rejoice?_____

_____

_____.

d. What is the meaning of the statement, "The barren woman is barren of her own works"? _____

_____

_____

_____

_____

_____

_____.

e. Based on Hebrews 4:10, what is a consequence for those who enter the rest of God?_____

_____

_____

_____

_____.

7. Read 1 Peter 1:6-8; John 16:7

a. We lack joy because we have problems. True or false? _____

_____.

b. In 1 Peter 1:6-8, what does the Bible tell us about joy? ____

_____

_____

_____

_____.

c. What do we need to do if we are not experiencing what the *King James Version* of 1 Peter 1:8 calls "joy unspeakable"?

_____

_____.

d. The blessings of the second covenant are available to us as believers, yet we are not experiencing them. Why?_____

_____

_____

_____ .

e. What will happen as long as we live in ignorance or neglect of the blessings that are ours under the covenant of grace?

_____ .

f. The author says that the Lord told her, "Frustration equals

_____ .

g. What does that mean? _____

_____

_____

_____

_____

_____

_____ .

h. Based on John 16:7, why did God give us His Holy Spirit?

_____ .

i. Why then do stubborn, independent people not receive the help they need?_____

_____

_____ .

j. How do we receive help — and thus avoid the frustration of works? _____ .

k. Why will only the humble among us do that?_____

_____

_____

_____.

8. Read 1 Peter 5:5-7; James 4:6,10

a. Based on 1 Peter 5:5-7, why is humility so important to God?

_____

_____

_____

_____

_____.

b. God's reasons for asking us to do things in the way He asks
are not to take anything away from us. Name two reasons He
asks us to do things His way._____

_____

_____

_____

_____.

c. Why must we always be on our guard against pride? _____

_____

_____.

d. According to James 4:6, why does God give us more and
more grace — power of the Holy Spirit? _____

_____

_____.

e. What does James go on to say in this same verse? _____

_____

_____

_____

_____

_____

_____.

f. In James 4:10, what does James then urge us, just as Peter did? _____

_____

_____

_____

_____.

g. How do we receive the grace of God?_____

_____

_____

_____

_____.

h. Why will proud people not do that?_____

_____

_____.

i. Why will only the humble do that? _____

_____

_____.

9. Read Psalm 127:1,2; Matthew 16:18; 1 Corinthians 3:9;
   Ephesians 2:20

a. What does Psalm 127:1 say about the building of a house?

_____

_____.

b. What is the first thing we should let God build in our lives?

_____.

c. In Matthew 16:18 Jesus said that He would build His Church. According to what Paul tells us in 1 Corinthians 3:9, who is that Church? _____.

d. Based on Ephesians 2:20, we are the _____, and Jesus is the _____.

e. How are we being built up?_____

_____.

f. The answer to how we get built is found in Paul's letter to the Galatians who needed to be reminded of _____

_____

_____.

10. Read Galatians 3:3-5; Ephesians 2:8,9; 1 Peter 2:5

a. What question do we need to ask ourselves that Paul was asking the "foolish," "senseless," and "silly" Galatians?_____

_____

_____

_____.

b. Just as we are saved by grace (God's unmerited favor) through faith, and not by works of the flesh, how do we need to learn to live?_____

_____

_____.

c. When we were saved, we were in no condition to help ourselves. What kind of condition are we in now that we have
been saved by grace through faith in the finished work of
Jesus Christ? _____

_____!

d. Why then do we keep trying to make things happen that are
never going to happen? _____

_____.

e. What is the only way we are ever going to be ". . . built [into]
a spiritual house, for a holy (dedicated, consecrated) priest-
hood, to offer up [those] spiritual sacrifices [that are] acceptable and pleasing to God through Jesus Christ"? _____

_____

_____

_____.

f. Since the flesh profits nothing, what causes us to grow up
into the perfection of Christ? _____.

11. Read Ephesians 4:12,13; Philippians 3:10; review Galatians 5:22,23

a. According to Ephesians 4:12, what was God's intention in
regard to the saints, His consecrated people? Why? _____

_____

_____

_____

_____

_____.

b. According to Ephesians 4:13, what does God want the Church of Jesus Christ to arrive at? _____

_____.

c. How is that state defined in verse 13? _____

_____

_____

_____

_____

_____.

d. Are you interested in being perfected? _____.

e. Based on Philippians 3:10 and Galatians 5:22,23, how does the author define being perfected or growing up in the Lord?

_____

_____

_____

_____

_____.

f. Since we cannot do that on our own, or change ourselves from what we are to what we want to be, what is the only thing we can do? _____

_____

_____

_____.

    g. What is the only way that can be done?_____

_____.

12. Read Colossians 1:4; John 6:28,29

    a. According to Colossians 1:4, what is faith? _____

_____

_____

_____

_____.

    b. Based on this verse, what is our only job? _____

_____

_____

_____.

    c. When the Holy Spirit convicts us of our sins, what is the first
thing we do? _____

_____

_____.

    d. What is the second thing we do? Why? _____

_____

_____

_____.

    e. According to John 6:29, the work that God requires of us is
to _____.

f. Believing requires that we _____
_____
_____ .

g. If we truly do that, we will not be_____
_____ . We will
quit trying to _____ and will
allow Him to _____
_____ .

13. Read Hebrews 3:4; Philippians 1:6; 1 John 1:9

a. _____ is the Master Builder. _____
is the Chief Cornerstone.

b. God is the One Who has to _____
_____ for the work of the Lord Jesus Christ.

c. What the apostle Paul was saying to us in Philippians 1:6 is
simply this: _____
_____
_____ !

d. What does that mean to us? _____
_____ .

e. Based on 1 John 1:9, what are we to do about our sins and
failures? _____
_____
_____
_____
_____ .

    f. What does that do for us? _____

_____

_____

_____.

14.   Read 1 Thessalonians 5:22-24

    a. What are God's instructions to us for finding peace and joy?

_____

_____

_____

_____.

    b. What does the author say that these verses are to us? _____

_____

_____

_____

_____

_____

_____.

    c. What then is our part? What is the work that we are to do? What does God require of us? _____

_____

_____

_____.

15.   Read Acts 20:32

    a. In this passage, what has God, the Master Builder, promised to do for us if we will allow Him to do so? _____

_____.

b. We have already discussed the first area in our lives in which we need to allow God to build. What is it? _____

_____.

c. What is the second area in our lives in which we need to allow God to build?_____.

d. What is the third area in our lives in which we need to allow God to build? _____.

16. Read Galatians 1:10; Philippians 2:7 KJV; Galatians 5:1; John 12:42,43

a. What choice made by the apostle Paul in his ministry must each of us make? _____

_____.

b. In Philippians 2:7 KJV we read that Jesus made Himself of no reputation. What does that mean to us?_____

_____

_____.

c. What will happen if it is our goal to try to build a name for ourselves? _____

_____

_____

_____.

d. If we are to be truly free in the Lord, we must do as Paul has told us in Galatians 5:1:_____

_____

_____

_____.

e. There is nothing the devil uses more to keep people out of the will of God than _____

_____.

f. The followers of Jesus have faced the choice between pleasing people and pleasing God since the very beginning. In the same way, what decision are we faced with today? _____

_____

_____

_____

_____

_____

_____

_____.

Chapter 4

The Arm of the Lord

1. Read John 12:38; Romans 12:1

    a. Explain how the arm of the Lord is in direct contrast to the arm of the flesh. _____

    _____

    _____

    _____.

    b. On what does each one of the two covenants depend?_____

    _____.

    c. What do we do under each one of the two covenants?_____

    _____

    _____

    _____

    _____

    _____.

    d. In Romans 12:1 what are we told to do? _____

    _____

    _____

    _____.

    e. According to the author, the Lord revealed three things to her that we must be in order to be filled with His Spirit and be pleasing to Him. What are they?_____

    _____.

f. How do we apply these three things to our lives? _____

_____

_____

_____

_____.

g. Name three things we must do to be pleasing to God. _____

_____

_____

_____

_____

_____

_____

_____

_____

_____.

h. In summary, to be pleasing to God, we must_____

_____

_____

_____.

2. Read Acts 7:9

a. What mistake did Joseph make in regard to the dream he had in which he saw himself being honored by all the members of his family, and why was what he did a mistake? _____

_____

_____

_____

_____

_____.

b. Why did God have to spend several years doing a work in Joseph before He could use him to fulfill His plan to bless him and his family and many, many others? _____

_____

_____.

c. What mistake do we make that young Joseph also made? __

_____

_____

_____

_____

_____

_____.

d. What was the result of the rashness of Joseph and his brothers?

_____

_____

_____.

e. What must we go through if we are going to enjoy the fullness of God in our lives? _____

_____.

f. What happens when all of the people and things we have been leaning on are stripped away from us? _____

_____

_____.

g. As in the case of Joseph, God wants us to depend upon ____
_____ and not
_____.

h. If it is not wrong to ever seek advice from others, why must
we be careful when we do so? _____
_____
_____.

i. What is the difference between most birds and eagles? ____
_____
_____.

j. What must each of us decide in reference to birds and eagles?
_____
_____
_____
_____.

k. If we want to be an eagle, we must _____
_____.

l. Joseph had to face hard, lonely times in his life, especially
during the period he spent in prison in a foreign country.
Despite all the adversity that came against him, what do the
Scriptures say about his situation? _____.

3. Read Acts 7:10; Psalm 75:6; Romans 8:31

a. Based on Acts 7:10, what did God do for Joseph, just as He
will do for us? _____
_____

_____

_____

_____.

b. Based on Psalm 75:6, how do we overcome adversity and opposition and gain favor and promotion? _____

_____

_____.

c. Based on Romans 8:31, why can no devil or person on earth prevent us from receiving favor and promotion?_____

_____

_____

_____.

d. If God's criteria for using people is not their talents, gifts, and abilities, what kind of people is He looking for? _____

_____.

e. If that is true, what then should you do to become successful in your life?_____

_____

_____

_____

_____

_____.

4. Read Genesis 50:18-20; review Romans 8:28

a. Based on Romans 8:28, whatever may have happened to us in the past, it does not have to dictate our future. Why? _____

_____

_____

_____.

b. Joseph's brothers meant evil to him, but God _____

_____.

c. Despite what others — even his own brothers — did to him, what two things did Joseph know that kept him from allowing himself to be filled with bitterness, resentment, and unforgiveness? _____

_____

_____

_____

_____

_____.

d. What did Joseph do that we need to do? _____

_____

_____.

5. Read Isaiah 40:6-8

a. The author says that when God called her into the ministry she did not have the kind of personality needed to minister, but what happened? _____

_____

_____.

b. Why should that be an encouragement to you? _____

_____

_____.

6. Read Philippians 3:3; review Isaiah 40:6-8

   a. Based on Philippians 3:3, we are going to either lean on the arm of the flesh or on the arm of the Lord. Explain. _____
   _____
   _____
   _____
   _____ .

   b. Why has the Lord told us through the prophet Isaiah not to trust in the flesh? _____
   _____
   _____ .

   c. Since we can put no confidence in the flesh, and apart from the Lord we can do nothing, what then must we do? _____
   _____
   _____
   _____ .

7. Read Proverbs 3:6; review Philippians 3:10; read Psalm 27:4; review Psalm 16:11; Ephesians 4:13; read Ephesians 6:4 KJV; Proverbs 22:6 KJV

   a. Based on Proverbs 3:6, what does it mean to acknowledge the Lord in all our ways? _____
   _____
   _____
   _____ .

   b. Based on Philippians 3:10, what does God want for us?____
   _____

_____

_____.

c. Based on Psalm 27:4 and 16:11, what one thing should we seek after? Why? _____

_____

_____.

d. What happens when we seek God's face (His Presence) to get to know our wonderful, loving heavenly Father better? ____

_____

_____.

e. Based on Ephesians 4:13, what is God waiting for us to do as His children?_____

_____.

f. Based on Ephesians 6:4 KJV and Proverbs 22:6 KJV, God is training us up, His children, in the way we _____ go — not the way we_____to go, but the way we _____ go.

8. Read James 4:13-15; Proverbs 16:18

a. According to James 4:13-15, instead of talking about our own plans, what should we say? _____

_____

_____.

b. What should we learn to want more than our own will? ___

_____.

c. If we want something and God says no, although it may hurt our feelings and be hard for us to accept, it will be_____

_____.

d. What is wrong with making our own plans and expecting God to bless them?_____

_____

_____

_____.

e. What does Proverbs 16:18 say about pride and a haughty spirit?

_____.

f. What is the key to the abundant, joyful, peaceful life Jesus died to give us? _____.

g. Why do we need to learn to humble ourselves under the mighty hand of God? _____

_____.

h. What is one way we humble ourselves? _____

_____

_____.

i. It honors God when we _____
Him. When we honor Him, He _____
us — and frequently gives us _____

_____!

j. The real issue here is _____.

9. Read 2 Kings 4:1-7; Galatians 2:20; review Philippians 1:6

    a. What is the key to value and worth? _____
        _____.

    b. Like the poor widow in 2 Kings 4:1-7, what is the first step to
        fullness? _____.

    c. We are empty vessels. What then is the only thing of value
        any of us has in us? _____
        _____
        _____
        _____.

    d. What do we have to offer God? _____.

    e. What value do we have? _____
        _____.

    f. Why is there nothing of value or worth in our flesh? _____
        _____
        _____.

    g. In Galatians 2:20, what did the apostle Paul say about the life
        he lived in the body? _____
        _____
        _____
        _____.

    h. Although it may seem as though reaching the place you
        desire is taking forever, what does Philippians 1:6 say about
        the good work that the Lord has begun in us? _____
        _____

_____

_____

_____

_____.

i. What will we be like if we press on and are sincere about spiritual maturity? _____

_____

_____

_____

_____.

j. What must we do to know and experience what God can do?

_____

_____

_____

_____

_____.

10. Read 2 Chronicles 20:1,4-6,10-12

a. In verse 12 of this passage, what three important statements do we see that apply to us today as much as they did to the people of Judah who faced overpowering enemies? _____

_____

_____

_____

_____.

b. When is the Lord free to move on our behalf, as He did for the people in this story?_____

_____

_____

_____

_____.

c. Why does it sometimes seem that God is not moving in our lives? _____

_____.

d. What is the reason that God may not be taking control of our situation? _____.

11. Read 2 Chronicles 20:13-18; review 20:12; Psalm 46:10 KJV; read Isaiah 40:31; Numbers 10:35; Philippians 2:10,11

a. According to 2 Chronicles 20:12, what three things must we do before we begin to shout what we read in verse 15, "O God, the battle is not mine, but Yours"? _____

_____

_____

_____

_____

_____.

b. When will God begin to give us His instructions for what to do? _____

_____.

c. Often His instructions to us will be what He told the people in the passage in 2 Chronicles 20:17: _____

_____.

d. Based on Numbers 10:35, what does the author say should be our war cry? _____ _____ !

e. Based on Philippians 2:10,11, what do we need to remember about the Lord? _____ _____ _____ _____ _____ .

f. In verse 17 of the passage in 2 Chronicles 20, what directions did God begin to give to His people through His prophet? _____ _____ _____ .

g. Why were they not to be afraid or dismayed? _____ _____ .

h. Faced with their enemies, what position did the people of God take in their situation that should be our position today? _____ _____ _____ .

i. We need to spend more time in worship and praise and less time in _____, _____, and _____.

j. We need to remember that God _____ the proud, but _____to the humble.

12. Review 1 Peter 5:5; read 2 Corinthians 4:4

    a. The world says,_____

      _____but that

      statement is totally _____.

    b. The Bible tells us God helps those who _____

      _____ in the sense

      that we are to _____

      _____

      _____

      _____, but on Him.

    c. Saying that God helps those who help themselves is not only unscriptural, but misleading. Why? _____

      _____

      _____

      _____

      _____.

    d. Satan, the god of this world's system, would like nothing better than for us to_____

      _____

      _____

      _____.

    e. If God does not help those who help themselves, who does He help? _____

      _____

      _____.

13. Read Deuteronomy 33:27

    a. Based on this verse, what does the author say that we should feel when we sing that old hymn, "Leaning on the Everlasting Arms"?_____

    _____

    _____.

    b. What should we experience? What decision should we make? _____

    _____

    _____.

14. Read 2 Chronicles 32:7,8; Jeremiah 17:5-8

    a. Based on 2 Chronicles 32:7,8, rather than looking at our past failures, our present fallacies, or our future fears, we should be _____

    _____

    _____.

    b. We should be reminding ourselves that no matter how many problems may be facing us, _____

    _____

    _____.

    c. In Jeremiah 17:5-8 we read that those who put their trust in the arm of the flesh are cursed with great evil. Explain. ____

    _____

    _____

    _____.

THE ARM OF THE LORD

d. According to that passage, those who put their trust in the arm of the Lord are blessed. Explain. _____

_____

_____

_____

_____

_____

_____

_____.

e. As we have already seen, we are not to lean on the arm of flesh, but on the arm of the Lord. To review, what does that mean? _____

_____.

f. Like Jesus, we need to _____ people, but not _____ourselves to them.

15. Read John 2:23-25

a. Although Jesus loved people, especially His disciples, why did He not put His trust in them?_____

_____.

b. That does not mean He had no trust in His relationship with them. What does that mean?_____

_____

_____

_____

_____.

c. Many times why do we become devastated when we form relationships with people? Explain. _____

_____

_____

_____

_____

_____

_____

_____.

d. Even in the best of human relationships we sometimes say and do things that hurt one another. Why does that happen?

_____.

e. Instead of placing our trust in the weak arm of the flesh, we should place it only in _____

_____.

f. What happens when we expect things from people they are not able to give us?_____

_____.

The Warfare of Rest

1. Read Hebrews 4:3; 2 Timothy 3:1-5,11-14; 4:2-5

    a. What does Hebrews 4:3 say about those of us ". . . who have believed (adhered to and trusted in and relied on God). . ."?

    _____

    _____ .

    b. In the warfare of rest, how do we defeat what the devil is trying to do in our life? _____

    _____ .

    c. Believers operate from a different world than that of unbelievers. Explain. _____

    _____ .

    d. Based on 2 Timothy 3:1, what kind of times are we in? _____

    _____

    _____ .

    e. What do verses 2 through 5 of 2 Timothy chapter 3 describe?

    _____

    _____ .

    f. In verse 11 of that chapter, after describing the persecutions and sufferings he endured, what does Paul then state about them?_____

    _____ .

    g. In chapter 4, what does Paul start to explain that is based on the passage in 2 Timothy chapter 3?_____

_____

_____

_____.

h. People who have "itching ears" in the church today won't lis-
    ten to teaching that doesn't suit them. What do they do
    instead? _____

    _____

    _____

    _____.

i. It is very dangerous to not listen to _____ —
    to _____ and _____based
    on God's Word!

j. In verse 5 of 2 Timothy chapter 4, Paul tells us what our
    response is to be to all the trouble in the world, all the trou-
    ble in our lives, the people that are hard to deal with or hard
    to bear. Based on that Scripture, our response to trouble is to
    be, _____

    _____!

k. When trouble starts in someone's life, and they react immedi-
    ately in the flesh instead of seeking the Lord for direction, the
    author calls this _____

    _____.

l. When trouble starts, sometimes God has us do such things as
    rebuke devils, fast, get people from church to pray with us
    and pull strongholds down, but what should we do first?

_____

_____

_____.

m. What must we remember in times of trouble? _____

_____

_____

_____.

2. Read Ephesians 6:13; Mark 8:22-25; John 9:1-7; Mark 10:46-52

   a. Based on Ephesians 6:13, what things are we to do when faced with challenges? _____

_____

_____.

   b. But what must we realize about crises? _____

_____

_____

_____.

   c. What is the reason that the solution to one crisis may not work the second time? _____

_____

_____

_____

_____.

   d. The passages in Mark chapter 8, John chapter 9, and Mark chapter 10 show how God uses _____methods for _____ people and in _____situations.

e. It was not any of the methods Jesus used that opened the blind eyes of these men in these passages so they could see. The thing that brought their healing was _____ _____.

f. The different methods were simply the different means used by Jesus to _____ _____.

g. The key to unleashing the power of God is _____.

3. Read Hebrews 4:2,3; 11:6; review Psalm 91:1

a. According to Hebrews 4:2, why didn't the message of glad tidings the Israelites heard benefit them? _____ _____ _____ _____ _____ _____ _____.

b. Whatever the Lord may lead us to do in order to release our faith and activate the power of God on our behalf, it will do us no good if we do not remain in the rest of God. Why? _____ _____ _____.

c. What does Hebrews 11:6 tell us? _____ _____.

d. According to Hebrews 4:2,3, rest is a _____.
The author believes that it is the_____
_____ spoken of in Psalm 91:1. That
secret place is _____
_____.

e. Why can we relax and be secure when we are in that secret
place?_____
_____
_____.

4. Read Exodus 33:12-14; review Psalm 91:1

a. When Moses complained to God that He had not let him
know whom He was going to send with him on his mission,
he asked Him to show him His way so He could get to know
Him better. According to this passage, what did the Lord do?
_____
_____.

b. This was considered by God to be a great privilege. To Him,
it was _____.

c. What was true for Moses is true for us. As much as we would
like to know God's plans and ways for us, all we really need
to know is that _____
_____.

d. What should we do if things don't work out the way we want
them to? _____
_____.

e. What must we remember if our plan is ruined? _____

_____

_____

_____

_____

_____.

f. What do we often do when things don't work out just as we want them to? _____.

g. Too often in the midst of our troubles what do we do wrong?

_____.

h. Instead of getting all upset and rebuking the devil every time something goes wrong, what does the author suggest we should do?_____

_____

_____

_____

_____.

5. Review Psalm 91; read Exodus 15:26

a. Of whom do verses 1 and 2 of Psalm 91 speak? _____

_____

_____

_____

_____

_____.

b. What is listed in the rest of the psalm? _____

_____

_____.

c. In *The Amplified Bible* there is a footnote at the bottom of the page on which Psalm 91 appears, which says that the promises of this whole psalm are dependent upon meeting exactly the conditions of the first two verses. Basically, what are the conditions of these first two verses? _____

_____.

d. According to the author, from what do we need to be delivered? _____

_____

_____

_____

_____

_____.

e. We need to remember that the _____ of the Lord depend upon the_____ of the Lord, which is always accompanied by the _____ _____ of the Lord.

6. Review John 14:27; read John 20:19,21,26; Psalm 42:5,11

a. What was the gift Jesus said He was leaving His disciples just before He was to go to the cross? _____

_____.

b. After His resurrection, what was the first thing He said to them each time He appeared to them? _____!

c. Obviously, what does Jesus intend for His followers to do despite what may be going on around them at the time? ____ _____.

d. Simply stated, what was He saying to His disciples — and to us? _____ _____ _____.

e. According to Psalm 42:5 and 11, what do we need to do when we begin to become cast down and disquieted within? ____ _____ _____ _____.

f. When we begin to lose our_____, we need to remember our_____.

7. Read Ephesians 2:4-6; 1:20; Colossians 3:1; Hebrews 1:3,13; 8:1; 10:12; 12:2; 1 Peter 3:22; Revelation 4:2

a. Our place is in Christ. Where is He according to Ephesians 1:20? _____ _____.

b. If we are in Him, and He is seated, then where should we be? _____.

8. Review Hebrews 1:3,13

    a. In this passage, we not only see the nature of Jesus as _____
        _____, and the role of Jesus as
        _____,
        we also see the place of Jesus — _____
        _____.

    b. It was _____Who made the devil into a
        _____.

9. Read Revelation 20:10

    a. How do we vocalize authority over the devil? _____
        _____.

    b. But at the same time, what do we need to recognize?_____
        _____
        _____
        _____.

    c. We are the Body of Christ, which includes His feet. What
        does that mean? _____
        _____
        _____
        _____
        _____
        _____
        _____
        _____
        _____.

10. Read Hebrews 10:12,13; 9:24; Exodus 28:35

  a. As we have already seen, Christ is seated in heavenly places and we are seated there with Him. According to Hebrews 10:12,13, what is He waiting for? _____

  _____

  _____.

  b. Under the old covenant, why were there no chairs in the earthly Holy of Holies?_____

  _____

  _____.

  c. Based on Hebrews 9:24, when would the Sabbath rest for God's people be instituted? _____

  _____

  _____

  _____.

  d. What did the Jewish high priest have to be doing all the time he was in the earthly Holy of Holies? _____

  _____.

  e. Under the old covenant, the covenant of works, the high priest had to keep moving while in the Holy of Holies; he was not allowed to sit down and rest. But once Jesus (our High Priest) had finished the work of salvation through His shed blood, when He entered into heaven what did His Father say to Him? _____

  _____.

f. That is the same message God is giving us today. What does He want us to know that is part of our inheritance as saints of the Lord?_____

_____

_____.

g. Now instead of running around trying to please God and win His favor through works of the flesh, what can we do? ____

_____

_____.

11. Read Matthew 11:28,29; Mark 4:39 KJV

a. Based on this passage in Matthew 11, how does God want us to enter His rest? _____

_____

_____.

b. What does finding rest, relief, ease, refreshment, recreation, and blessed quiet for the soul mean? _____

_____

_____

_____

_____

_____

_____

_____

_____.

c. Based on Mark 4:39 KJV, when something goes wrong, instead of getting all upset and just rebuking the devil, what can we do? _____

_____

_____

_____

_____.

d. The author says that the Lord has taught her in trying times we can possess our soul. In doing this what are we actually doing? _____

_____.

12. Read Luke 21:19; review Psalm 91:11; read Psalm 37:23 KJV

a. According to Luke 21:19, how will we win the true life of our souls?_____

_____.

b. The author says that all of us need to learn not to _____

_____

_____

_____.

c. If we have done our best, God will _____

_____.

d. We often become so upset over what happened, we fail to realize _____

_____.

e. To summarize, we need to refuse to get wild. We need to refuse to allow our mind, will, and emotions to rule our spirit. In our patience we need to _____

    _____

    _____.

13. Read Ephesians 4:26,27

    a. As we saw happen to the author, what sometimes happens when someone we love wants us to do something we don't want to do? _____

        _____.

    b. Why do we need to learn to "go with the flow" and not cause so many problems over things that don't really matter? ____

        _____

        _____

        _____.

    c. Instead of making mountains out of molehills, blowing things up all out of proportion, and making major issues out of minor situations that are of no real importance whatsoever, what do we need to learn to do? _____

        _____

        _____

        _____

        _____.

    d. What happens when we get all upset about unimportant things? _____

_____

_____.

e. It is amazing what the Lord would deliver us from, sover-
    eignly and supernaturally, if we would _____

    _____.

f. Does learning to control our emotions instead of letting them
    control us mean that we are to have no feelings? Explain. __

    _____

    _____

    _____.

14. Read Philippians 1:28; Romans 4:21

a. According to Philippians 1:28, what is the clear sign, proof,
    seal, token, and evidence to our enemies of their defeat and
    destruction and of our deliverance and salvation? _____

    _____.

b. What is the sign to the devil that he cannot control us?_____

    _____

    _____.

c. Why then does our deliverance sometimes seem to take so
    long? _____

    _____.

d. The devil does not want us to think we can relax, rest, and
    enjoy life while we are having problems. He wants us to ___

    _____

    _____

_____

_____.

    e. The author says that when the devil sends people to ask us what we are going to do in times of adversity, our answer should be_____

_____

_____

_____

_____.

15. Read Psalm 94:12,13

    a. How does God use the events and people of our lives? _____

_____

_____.

    b. For what purpose and goal do we think God wants to empower us?_____

_____.

    c. The Lord has a much greater goal and purpose in mind for empowering us. What is it? _____

_____

_____

_____

_____

_____

_____.

d. Why is God working in our lives to discipline, instruct, and teach us? _____

_____.

e. With that power, what are we able to do? _____

_____

_____

_____

_____.

f. In review: Seated with Christ at the right hand of God in heavenly places, trusting not in the arm of the flesh but in the arm of the Lord, what can we truly be? _____

_____.

PART 2

Cast All Your Care

Introduction

"Casting the whole of your care [all your anxieties, all your worries, all your concerns, once and for all] on Him, for He cares for you affectionately and cares about you watchfully."

1 Peter 5:7

Are you enjoying the peace that results from casting all your care on God? You may be in the habit of taking on those cares and trying to handle them yourself. As long as that is true, you will be frantic, erratic, and frenzied in your approach to life.

Cares and concerns seem to be a part of life. You can triumph in the midst of them by remaining calm.

God wants to bless you with peace, but His hands are tied until you make some adjustments. You cannot handle your own problems; no one can. We are not built for it. The devil wants you to be weighed down and burdened with care. He wants you to think about your problems, worry about them, try to reason them out and solve them yourself. God wants you to cast all of your care on Him and enter into a lifestyle of peace and joy.

God doesn't want you to be anxious because it prevents you from receiving and doing all He has planned for you. He loves you and wants to bless you and has provided ways for you to be carefree.

I believe this next section of the guidebook will give you the insight you need to help you deal with several issues relating to your care. Every day is a wonderful gift from God in which He has exciting things in store for you. All you have to do is trust Him. He is faithful, and you can depend on Him to take care of you. As you give your care to Him, He will give you something in return — the full and abundant life that He wills for us through His Son Jesus Christ.

1. Review 1 Peter 5:7

   a. Based on 1 Peter 5:7, why does the Bible say we can cast all our care on God? _____
   _____.

   b. What does that mean? _____
   _____.

   c. In order for Him to do that, what must we do?_____
   _____
   _____.

   d. In His Word, what does the Lord promise us if we will give Him our care? _____
   _____.

2. Read Isaiah 61:1-3

   a. In this passage, what does God promise us? _____
   _____
   _____
   _____.

   b. What is one of the positive exchanges God promises to make?
   _____.

   c. What happens if we do not give God our ashes?_____
   _____.

    d. What must we do if we are to receive the blessings God wants to bestow upon us? _____

_____.

    e. _____ for

_____ — that's quite an exchange!

3.   Review John 10:10

    a. What did we learn in Part 1 of this book? _____

_____

_____

_____

_____

_____.

    b. In Part 2 we are going to deal with_____.

_____.

Chapter
6

He Careth for You

1. Review Psalm 91; read John 15:4

    a. As we have seen, what do verses 3 through 16 of this psalm contain? _____
        _____.

    b. What must we do to receive the blessings promised us in this psalm? _____
        _____
        _____
        _____
        _____.

    c. There are three aspects of Psalm 91:1,2 that determine our ability to receive God's richest blessings. What is the first one and what does it mean? _____
        _____
        _____
        _____.

    d. What is the second one and what does it mean? _____
        _____
        _____
        _____
        _____
        _____
        _____.

e. What is the third one and what does it mean? _____

_____

_____

_____

_____

_____

_____.

2. Review Psalm 91:3-8; 91:1,2

What are the wonderful promises the Lord will fulfill for us when
we do the things required of us in verses 1 and 2? _____

_____

_____

_____

_____

_____

_____

_____

_____.

3. Review Psalm 91:9-16; read Luke 10:19

a. What does *The Amplified Bible* version make very clear about
this passage of Psalm 91?_____

_____

_____

_____.

b. Luke 10:19 describes our place in God. We believers are ____

_____

_____

_____.

c. We are also in a position of _____

and _____with God.

d. Saying we have angelic protection does not mean we will never have any trials or afflictions. What does it mean?_____

_____

_____

_____

_____.

e. What is one important thing we must learn about this angelic protection and deliverance?_____

_____.

f. In verses 15 and 16 of Psalm 91, what does the Lord promise?

_____

_____

_____

_____

_____.

g. Based on what the Lord promises, what is the pattern? _____

_____

_____

_____

_____.

4. Read Psalm 27:4-6

    a. Based on this passage, what does the author do that we
        should do when things start to go wrong in our life? _____

        _____

        _____

        _____

        _____

        _____

        _____

        _____.

    b. If we worship and seek God, what does He do? _____

        _____.

5. Read Psalm 63:1-7

    a. Based on this passage, how does the author describe a shad-
        ow? _____

        _____

        _____

        _____.

    b. In the same way how does that relate to us if we are to remain
        under the shadow of God's wings? _____

        _____

        _____

        _____

        _____.

    c. Why should we choose to remain under the shadow of God's
        wings rather than to walk out from under them? _____

_____

_____

_____

_____.

d. The wise thing is not only to choose to stay under the shadow of the Almighty, but to _____

_____.

e. The dividing lines between lanes and the signposts along the road are put there for our benefit and protection. In the spiritual realm, what are the "lines and signs" that keep us on the way of the Lord and out of danger? _____

_____.

f. What will happen as long as we place our trust and confidence in the Lord? _____

_____

_____.

6. Review Philippians 4:6,7

a. In this passage the apostle Paul does not say, "Pray and worry." Instead, he says,_____

_____.

b. Why are we to pray and not worry? _____

_____

_____.

c. What are we supposed to do when the devil tries to give us care? _____

_____ .

d. How do we do that? Why? _____

_____

_____

_____

_____ .

e. What are we doing if we pray about something and then keep on worrying about it?_____

_____

_____

_____

_____ .

f. Why do many people operate at zero power level spiritually?

_____

_____

_____

_____ .

g. Why should we not worry? _____

_____

_____

_____

_____

_____ .

7. Review Hebrews 4:3

   a. Based on this verse, if we are not at rest, we are not _____
      _____ . Why? _____
      _____ .

   b. If we are truly believing God and trusting the Lord, what has
      happened to us? _____
      _____ .

   c. If we have entered into God's rest, we have prayed and cast
      our care upon the Lord and are now _____
      _____
      _____ .

8. Read Romans 5:2-4

   a. It is easy to say, "Don't worry." What does it require to actu-
      ally do that? _____ .

   b. What does it take for a person to fully overcome the habit of
      worry, anxiety, and fear and develop the habit of peace, rest,
      and hope? _____
      _____ .

   c. That's why it is so important to continue to have faith and
      trust in God in the very midst of trials and tribulations, to
      resist the temptation to give up and quit when the going gets
      rough — and keeps on getting rougher over a long period of
      time. What is the Lord building in us in those hard, trying
      times? _____
      _____

_____

_____

_____.

d. When we are in the midst of battle against our spiritual enemy, every round we go through produces valuable _____ and _____. Each time we endure an attack, we become _____

_____.

e. If we hang in there and refuse to give up, what will be the result? _____

_____.

f. When that happens, we will have reached _____

_____.

g. We should learn to pray to God and cast our care upon Him — _____. We need to learn to endure our personal suffering _____.

h. There is a time to share what we are going through, and there is a time to keep things between us and God. Often we talk so much about "what we are going through" that_____

_____

_____.

i. What does God do with things that Satan intends for our harm? _____.

9. Read Isaiah 53:7

   a. In the Old Testament, what did the prophet Isaiah foretell about what would happen when the Messiah was led away to be sacrificed for the sins of the world? _____

   _____

   _____

   _____.

   b. What happens to us in trying times? _____

   _____

   _____

   _____.

10. Read Philippians 4:11

    a. As he stated in Philippians 4:11, what ability did Paul have?

    _____

    _____.

    b. What did he know how to do that gave him that ability?

    _____

    _____

    _____.

    c. In spite of all the challenges he faced and all the hardships he had to go through, what did Paul know? _____

    _____

    _____.

    d. If that is not true of you, what did Paul say that will keep you from becoming discouraged? _____

_____

_____.

e. If we do not have it yet, sooner or later we can begin to develop the ability to be content in whatever state we may find ourselves. How? _____

_____

_____

_____

_____.

11. Read Proverbs 3:5,6

a. As we travel down the road of life, how will the devil try to distract us to keep us from making progress toward our goal?

_____

_____

_____.

b. But what can happen if we keep within the lines and obey the signs along the way? _____

_____

_____.

c. Instead of trying to figure out everything for ourselves, what should we do?_____

_____

_____.

d. How can we tell when we have begun to cross over the boundary? _____

_____.

e. Whatever the problem may be that is causing us to lose our peace, what should we do about it? _____

_____

_____

_____

_____.

f. In the passage from Proverbs 3:5,6 what are we told to do?

_____

_____.

g. As we have seen, faith is the leaning of the _____

_____

on God in absolute_____

and_____in His power, wisdom, and goodness.

h. What does God mean when He says that we are to lean on Him? _____

_____

_____.

i. What is always a sign we are getting over the line and headed for trouble? _____

_____.

12. Review Matthew 6:25-33

a. What does Jesus talk to us directly about in this passage?

_____

_____.

b. What should we do every time we are tempted to worry or be anxious about anything in life? _____

_____ .

c. In verse 25 what does Jesus command us specifically to do?

_____

_____

_____ .

d. Why should we quit torturing ourselves with negative thoughts and feelings? _____

_____

_____ .

e. In verse 26 Jesus commands us to look at the birds of the air. What does He want us to see and understand? _____

_____

_____

_____

_____ .

f. In verse 32 Jesus assure us_____

_____

_____

_____

_____ .

g. Finally, in verse 33 Jesus gives us the key to living in the peace of the Lord. What is it? _____

_____

_____

_____
_____.

h. What is the reason that we worry and fret and live in anxiety and fear? _____
_____
_____
_____.

i. As the Body of Christ, we are supposed to seek God, not the answer to our problems. What are we promised if we will seek Him and His righteousness? _____
_____.

j. Instead of spending all our time seeking the perfect mate or a happy home or a successful career or ministry, what are we told to do in the Word of God? _____
_____
_____
_____
_____.

13. Read 1 Peter 5:6,7 KJV; review Psalm 27:4-6; 91; Matthew 6:25-34; read Psalm 37

   Let's take a moment to review some of the things we have learned so far.

   a. In Psalm 27 we saw the psalmist had the right idea when he wrote the one thing he asked of the Lord was _____
   _____
   _____.

b. What did we see in Psalm 91?_____

_____

_____

_____

_____

_____.

c. What did we see in Matthew 6:25-33 that we are not to seek
after? _____

_____

_____

_____.

d. What did we see in verse 34 of that passage? _____

_____

_____

_____

_____

_____.

e. What are we told in the passage in 1 Peter 5:6,7 KJV?_____

_____

_____

_____

_____.

f. What are we told several times in Psalm 37? What are we to
do instead? _____

_____

_____

_____

_____

_____

_____.

14.   Read Psalm 18:1-3; 61:2; 62:2; Ephesians 6:10-17; Psalm 125:1,2; review Psalm 37:17.

    a. In Psalm 18:1-3, 61:2 and 62:2, David said God only was his Rock and Fortress. That should be our testimony also. In that case, Who should our Rock of security be? _____

       _____.

    b. A rock is a type of a sure foundation. When the waters of trial threaten to rise up and overwhelm us, what should we do?

       _____

       _____.

    c. David also called the Lord his Fortress. What is a fortress?

       _____

       _____

       _____

       _____

       _____

       _____

       _____.

    d. What else did David also call the Lord? _____

       _____

       _____

       _____

_____
_____.

e. What do Psalm 125:1,2 and Psalm 37:17 tell us about where
    God is? _____
    _____
    _____.

f. Based on those passages, what is God doing for us? _____
    _____
    _____
    _____
    _____.

g. The devil is against us, but God is _____us, and
    _____ us, and _____ us, and_____us.

h. Because He cares for us, what does God do for us?_____
    _____
    _____
    _____
    _____.

Chapter 7

Cast Your Care, Not Your Responsibility

1. Read 1 Peter 5:6,7; review John 6:28,29

   a. It is important that we learn to cast our _____, but not our _____.

   b. So often what do we do instead?_____
   _____
   _____.

   c. There is a difference between _____
   _____ and _____
   _____.

   d. As Jesus told us in John 6:28,29, what is our first responsibility as believers? _____.

   e. Why should that not be a struggle for us? _____
   _____
   _____
   _____.

   f. To summarize, what is one thing God has told us to do? ___
   _____
   _____.

2. Read Matthew 11:12; Philippians 3:12

   a. Why does the author say that *casting* is a violent word?____
   _____
   _____
   _____

_____
_____.

b. In Matthew 11:12, what did Jesus say about the Kingdom of
    God? _____
    _____
    _____
    _____.

c. In what way, then, and about what are we going to have to get
    violent? _____
    _____
    _____
    _____
    _____.

d. Where is part of that violence expressed? _____
    _____
    _____
    _____
    _____.

e. In Philippians 3:12, what did the apostle Paul say he did?
    _____
    _____
    _____.

f. Sometimes we have to get angry enough to _____
    _____
    _____
    _____ that try to keep us from enjoying

_____

_____

_____ .

g. Often we get mad at other people when we should be mad at

_____ .

h. Just as anger at Satan can be a form of righteous violence, so can be casting our care on the Lord. Explain. _____

_____

_____

_____

_____ .

i. What can we do when Satan tries to force us to carry a bur-den of care? _____

_____

_____

_____ !

j. Everyone has their own set of problems, but has become very good at hiding them. How can we be free of that kind of cha-rade? _____

_____

_____

_____

_____ .

k. What do we need to do to settle once and for all the spiritual issues that are keeping us from walking in the fullness of joy, peace, and rest the Lord intends for us? _____

_____

_____.

l. The Bible says we are to cast all our care upon God. What does the Greek word translated *care* in 1 Peter 5:7 mean?

_____

_____

_____

_____.

m. Why does the devil try to give us care? _____

_____.

n. What do we need to know in order to cast our care, but not our responsibility? _____

_____.

3. Read 1 Peter 5:7 WORRELL

a. According to the footnote in the *Worrell New Testament,* what does the Greek tense of 1 Peter 5:7 indicate?_____

_____

_____.

b. The footnote continues, "This, in a sense, is done when ___

_____

_____

_____

_____.

c. Then the footnote tells us, "When one puts the whole management of his life in God's hands, he may _____

_____

_____

_____

_____.

d. What sin are we often guilty of, which causes many problems? _____.

e. A desire for independence is a sign of _____

_____.

f. Why do we sometimes not want our heavenly Father's help when He tries to help us? What is the result? _____

_____

_____.

g. If we want to experience the peace of the Lord, what must we do? _____

_____.

h. Based on Worrell's study notes, what is the way we overcome a spirit of independence? _____

_____

_____.

i. So what is our first responsibility? What is our second responsibility? _____

_____

_____
_____
_____.

4. Read John 16:7,8

    a. We must learn to distinguish between _____ part
        and _____ part — and then leave _____
        _____ to Him, refusing to _____
        _____.

    b. People cannot change people. Only _____
        can change people.

    c. According to the Bible, Who convicts and convinces of sin
        and of righteousness? _____.

    d. Like the author, when we try to convict others of what we
        think are their sins and try to convince them of our right-
        eousness, why are we always in such a struggle?_____
        _____
        _____.

    e. In addition to submitting ourselves entirely to the Lord, trust-
        ing Him to work out things for us as He knows best, what else
        must we do? _____
        _____
        _____
        _____.

5.   Read 1 Corinthians 2:16; Isaiah 55:8,9

   a. Based on these passages, it is not our job to give God _____
       _____, _____ or
       _____.

   b. In His Word, He makes it clear that He doesn't need us to
       _____ or tell Him _____
       _____.

   c. What is our job concerning this? _____
       _____
       _____
       _____
       _____
       _____

   d. God is God — and we aren't. Why do we need to simply rec-
       ognize that truth and trust ourselves to Him? _____
       _____
       _____.

   e. We are created in God's image, but He is still above us and
       beyond us. Since His thoughts and ways are higher than ours,
       what will He do if we will listen to Him and be obedient to
       Him? _____.

6.   Read Romans 9:20,21

   a. It is not our place to cross-examine God. Why not? _____
       _____
       _____.

b. What may be the reason God does not answer our prayers?

_____

_____.

c. What has been noted as the biggest problem for most Christians? _____

_____

_____.

d. What makes us think that what we are asking is God's will?

_____

_____

_____

_____.

e. Since many things in this life are not clearly laid out in Scripture, what must we have from the Lord to know whether they are His will for us or not? _____

_____.

f. Even if something is God's will for us, what must we also consider? What does that take on our part?_____

_____.

g. Like the author, why do we often struggle with these matters?

_____

_____

_____

_____

_____.

h. As the author realized about her prayers, too often what are our prayers, and what do we try to do through them? _____

_____

_____

_____ .

i. According to the author, the Lord showed her in His Word what the problem was that kept Him from answering her prayers as He promised. Like her, even though we are asking, what is our problem? _____

_____

_____ .

7. Read James 4:1-3

a. Based on this passage, why do we often get into struggles and strife?_____

_____

_____

_____ .

b. Based on the second part of this passage, as we already discussed, why do we not get our prayers answered even when we do ask?_____

_____

_____ .

c. Like the author, when we ask the Lord for something and we don't get it, it's not because He doesn't want to bless us or because He is holding out on us. What is the reason? _____

_____

_____
_____
_____.

8. Review Psalm 37:3-5; read Deuteronomy 8:19

   a. What has the author learned since the Lord spoke to her about what was wrong with the way she was praying? _____
   _____
   _____.

   b. How did she say that she prays if she is not sure what God's will is in a situation? _____
   _____
   _____
   _____
   _____
   _____
   _____
   _____.

   c. According to what she has learned about prayer, what should we seek first? _____
   _____
   _____
   _____
   _____
   _____.

d. What will happen if we seek God for money or things with-
    out seeking Him? _____

    _____.

e. If our _____does not

    go as deep as our _____,

    we only get in trouble.

f. What must happen in our lives for anything else to work
    properly? _____

    _____.

g. Literally any blessing of the Lord can get us in trouble if we
    don't keep our lives in balance and turn the blessing into a
    god. What must we do regularly to keep that from happen-
    ing? _____

    _____

    _____.

h. It is such a deliverance to turn the management of our life
    over to God. Does that mean we are to become passive and
    stop resisting the enemy Satan when he attacks us? Explain.

    _____

    _____

    _____.

i. What will happen if we wait on the Lord and listen to Him?

    _____

    _____

    _____

    _____

_____

_____

_____.

j. Although it is God's will to bless us, why does He not neces-
    sarily bless us on our terms? _____

    _____

    _____.

k. In all our seeking, struggling, and striving — even in prayer
    — why must we be careful not to give birth to Ishmaels?

    _____

    _____.

l. What should we do instead? Why?_____

    _____

    _____

    _____

    _____.

9. Read Isaiah 45:9-11; review Romans 9:20,21; read Ephesians
    2:10; 1 Corinthians 13:12

    a. We see that the passage in Isaiah 45:9-11 talks against ques-
        tioning God, and in Romans 9:20,21 we saw we are not to

        _____

        _____

        _____.

    b. Who can say why God puts us together the way He does? But
        He is the _____, and we are the

        _____.

c. Not only do we question God about why He made us the way He did, we also question Him about_____

_____.

d. As long as we argue with God and strive with our Maker, what will be the result? _____

_____.

e. Once we accept God's will, what will be the result? _____

_____

_____.

f. In Romans 9:21, when Paul asks whether the potter has the right to make one vessel for honorable use and another vessel for dishonorable use, does that mean dishonorable in God's eyes? Explain._____

_____

_____

_____

_____

_____.

g. We are where we are because God Himself has placed us there. Wherever He has placed us, what must we do? _____

_____

_____

_____

_____.

h. As long as we function in the position God has created us for, His _____. But the moment we get out of our God-ordained role, we are

_____

_____ .

i. Based on 1 Corinthians 13:12, what is the best answer to the question of why God does anything the way He does? _____

_____ .

j. It is not our job to question God, or even try to explain Him. It is our job to_____and

_____ Him and to

_____

_____upon Him.

10. Read 2 Timothy 4:5

a. As ministers of the Gospel of Jesus Christ, which is what we are all called to be, what are our basic duties or responsibilities? _____

_____

_____

_____

_____ .

b. When there is something that greatly concerns us, like the salvation of our spouse or children, what can happen? _____

_____

_____ .

c. Excessive prayer, especially in the area of spiritual warfare, can become _____

_____ .

d. In our prayers, as in every other aspect of our Christian life, we need not be afraid of_____

_____.

e. It is our responsibility to trust, to pray without worry, and to avoid works of the flesh. What happens when we go beyond that responsibility and start to pray and worry? _____

_____

_____

_____

_____.

11. Read Galatians 2:21 KJV

a. God is not against work. He is against _____.

b. What is the difference? _____

_____

_____

_____

_____

_____

_____

_____

_____

_____.

c. What happens when we do the work God has called us to do?

_____.

d. Physically we may be tired, but spiritually we are renewed and refreshed by the Spirit of the Lord. That is a good example of _____ _____ and _____ _____.

e. What works of the flesh are one of the biggest problems among God's people today? _____ _____ _____ _____.

f. As we have seen, what is the opposite of works? _____.

g. As long as we are trying to live the Christian life by works of the flesh, we are never going to be _____ _____.

h. Why does the devil try to use works of the flesh against us? _____ _____ _____ _____ _____.

i. Instead of trusting in the Lord and waiting for Him to move in His own way and timing, what does the devil want us to do? _____ _____ _____.

12. Read Genesis 16:5,6; 3:12

   a. In Part 1, we read how Sarah, despairing of ever having a child of her own in her old age, suggested to Abraham that he take her Egyptian maid Hagar as his "secondary wife" and have a child by her. What was Abraham's response? _____

   _____

   _____

   _____.

   b. In Genesis 16:5,6, what immediate consequences of that action do we see? _____

   _____

   _____

   _____.

   c. What did Sarah do in reaction to this situation? _____

   _____

   _____

   _____!

   d. In what way was Abraham to blame for this situation? _____

   _____

   _____

   _____.

   e. Instead of waiting for the Lord to supernaturally produce the promised heir, what was the result of Abraham and Sarah's foolish attempt to produce an heir on their own through totally human effort? _____

   _____

_____

_____ .

f. What was the reason that Abraham failed to fulfill his responsibility? _____

_____

_____

_____

_____ .

g. How is that often our problem? _____

_____

_____

_____

_____

_____

_____ .

h. When Hagar became pregnant and treated Sarah cruelly, how did Abraham again shift his responsibility? _____

_____

_____ .

i. In both cases, how did Abraham avoid his God-given responsibility? _____

_____ .

j. Based on Genesis 3:12, the same kind of thing happened with Adam in the Garden of Eden. Explain. _____

_____

_____
_____
_____
_____
_____
_____.

k. What job has the devil done on many men today? _____

_____
_____
_____
_____.

l. What change in this situation are we seeing? _____

_____
_____
_____
_____.

13. Read Colossians 4:17 NIV

a. In review, what are our first three duties or responsibilities?

_____
_____
_____.

b. What are our three final duties or responsibilities? _____

_____
_____
_____
_____.

14. Read John 2:5; 2:1-11; Galatians 6:9

    a. Based on the passage in John 1-11, the first rule of miracles is
    _____.

    b. If you are looking for a miracle in your life, what should you
    do? Based on Galatians 6:9, why should you do so? _____
    _____
    _____
    _____
    _____
    _____.

    c. Sometimes when things are not working out the way we
    think they should, or we are not receiving the answers to our
    prayers as quickly as we would like, we get the idea, "Well,
    since God's not doing anything, why should I? Why should I
    be obedient if it isn't producing results?" In such times we
    must realize that _____
    _____
    _____.

15. Read Psalm 139:15,16; John 5:17; Matthew 9:29 KJV

    a. In Psalm 139:15,16, the psalmist wrote that long before his
    actual appearance in this world, he was _____
    _____.

    b. What kind of work did God put together in the form of King
    David of Israel, just as He is putting together in our lives?
    _____.

c. David did not make his appearance in this world until ____
_____.

d. In the same way, when will God bring forth His perfect work
in us?_____
_____.

e. Even though it may seem God is doing nothing, He is_____
_____
_____. We may not
be able to hear it or see it, but we can accept it_____
_____.

f. Based on Matthew 9:29 KJV, at this very moment while you
are reading this book, God is at work in your life and in your
present situation, if you _____.

g. If you have cast your care upon the Lord and left it with Him
to handle, what is He doing right now? _____
_____
_____.

h. What does He want you to do? _____
_____
_____
_____.

i. How do you do that? _____
_____
_____
_____
_____.

16. Read Jeremiah 17:7,8; Ephesians 3:17; review Galatians 5:22,23; James 4:6

   a. What should we be doing while we are waiting on the Lord?
   _____.

   b. What should we be like? Why?_____
   _____
   _____
   _____
   _____
   _____.

   c. If we are firmly planted in Jesus Christ and deeply rooted in His love, what will we still do even though we may have all kinds of problems in our lives? _____
   _____
   _____
   _____.

   d. Why should we not think we have a license to be miserable and ugly when we are going through hard times?_____
   _____
   _____.

   e. In James 4:6 what does the Bible teach us about such "evil tendencies"? _____
   _____
   _____
   _____.

17. Read Hebrews 13:15; review Psalm 139:13-16

   a. In Psalm 139:15,16, what did we see that David acknowledged about God? _____

      _____

      _____.

   b. In verses 13 and 14 of that Psalm, for what did he praise the Lord? _____

      _____

      _____.

   c. Like David, what are we to do in the midst of our problems?

      _____

      _____

      _____

      _____

      _____.

   d. In summary, it is not our responsibility to worry and fret or try to play God by taking into our own hands things that should be left to Him alone. Instead, it is our responsibility to

      _____

      _____

      _____

      _____

      _____.

This Too Shall Pass

1. Read Genesis 4:14 KJV; Genesis 39 KJV; Revelation 1:1 KJV

   a. What prophetic word do we see in the beginning chapters of the book of Genesis? _____
   _____.

   b. In fulfillment of this word, the expression "it came to pass" is used hundreds of times throughout the *King James Version* of the Bible. What should that tell us? _____
   _____
   _____
   _____.

   c. Life is a continual process in which everything is constantly changing. If we can grasp that truth, how will it help us?
   _____
   _____
   _____
   _____
   _____
   _____
   _____.

   d. What does God want us to enjoy? _____
   _____.

2. Read Ecclesiastes 5:18

   a. Based on this verse, do you find enjoyment in your labor? Why or why not? _____

_____

_____.

b. The author says that the Lord showed her in our lives we are
always going to be _____

_____. As soon as we finish one,

_____

_____.

c. She says the Lord was teaching her that since we are going to
spend our entire lives waiting for something, we should ___

_____

_____.

d. What will happen if we don't do that? _____

_____.

3. Read Zecharaiah 4:10

a. Like the author, we may have hated the "day of small things"
and the hardships of early times while they were going on,
but now we see their value. Why were they important?_____

_____

_____

_____.

b. Why is it sad that today many times people give up in the
hard times? _____

_____.

c. It is easy to start something, but it is much harder to_____

_____.

d. In the beginning, we are filled with emotion, and usually have all kinds of enthusiastic support. Everybody cheers us on. But as the days go by and the great and glorious cause becomes a matter of daily, consistent hard work, what often happens to us? _____

_____

_____

_____.

e. That's when we have to decide if we are going to _____

_____.

That's when we have to realize _____

_____

_____.

f. In the meantime, what should we do? _____

_____.

4. Read Mark 9:2-6

a. In the Gospels we never find Jesus saying, "This is it!" Instead, what do we often find Him saying? _____

_____

_____.

b. Then what does He do? _____.

c. What is one of our problems in this area? _____

_____.

d. We like to think that things, especially pleasant things, are never going to change. When we win a victory, we like to think that is the end of our troubles, and we will never have to fight another battle. Why does the Lord try to tell us that is not so? _____

_____.

e. One season always leads to_____.

f. If the situation we are in at the moment is not very pleasant, it will at least _____

_____.

g. In the same way, a pleasant situation may have to change for a while so _____

_____.

h. What do trying times do for us? _____

_____

_____

_____

_____.

i. We have to grow and develop. Like all of God's children, we have to go through some _____

_____.

5. Read Hebrews 12:7-11

In verse 11 of this passage, what does the phrase "but afterwards" mean? _____

_____

_____

_____

_____ .

6. Review Psalm 91:14-16

    a. What three things does God promise us in this passage if we
        are in trouble?_____

        _____

        _____

        _____ .

    b. The author believes the message the Lord is giving us in these
        verses is simply this:_____

        _____

        _____

        _____

        _____

        _____

        _____ .

7. Read Mark 13:31

    a. God doesn't always change those people we want Him to
        change; instead, He often uses them to _____ .

    b. What we believe to be our worst enemy often, in actuality, is
        our _____ .

    c. What things does God use to change us?_____

        _____ .

d. Sometimes we need to look ahead with the eye of faith to __

_____

_____ .

e. When God is dealing with you, instead of looking at the training, correction, and discipline you are going through for the moment, what should you look at? _____

_____

_____ .

f. When you don't see the manifestation of your prayers, what should you do? _____

_____

_____

_____

_____ .

g. To review, when you are going through trying times, what should be your message to yourself? _____

_____ .

8. Read Ecclesiastes 3:1; Psalm 62:10; Proverbs 27:24; Philippians 3:13,14

a. What two lies does the devil offer us? _____

_____ .

b. Why are both of these lies untrue? _____

_____ .

c. What happens if we continue to believe God and place our trust in Him?_____

_____.

d. When we do have good things going on in our lives, does that mean that they will stay exactly the same forever? Explain.

_____

_____

_____

_____

_____.

e. The devil wants you to feel that things will never change, and if you believe his lies,_____

_____

_____.

f. Sometimes changes are exciting — sometimes they're hard. But Jesus never changes — and as long as we _____

_____, we will

_____the changes

in our life and continue _____

_____.

g. When the Bible tells us that we are not to set our hearts on the things of this world, what does it mean? _____

_____

_____.

h. As believers, to what is our attachment supposed to be? ___

    _____

    _____.

i. We are to enjoy what we have while we have it, but we are never to get to the point where we _____

    _____.

j. According to the author, what is one of the things the Lord is saying to us today?_____

    _____.

k. We must remember that we are_____
of what God has provided us, not _____.

l. Why must we not get attached to people or to things?_____

    _____

    _____.

m. There is a season in our lives, and when that season is over, what must we do? _____.

n. Too often what mistake do we make in this area? _____

    _____

    _____

    _____.

o. If God is done with something in your life, what should you do? _____

    _____

    _____

    _____

_____

_____ .

p. If God is no longer in something, you will no longer be happy in it. What then should you do? Why? _____

_____

_____

_____ .

9. Read Genesis 12:1-4

a. In this passage, what did God tell Abraham to do? _____

_____

_____ .

b. The author says that is what God did to her when He told her to leave a certain job. At one time in her life, that job was "it," but now the Lord was telling her _____

_____

_____ .

c. Does that mean it was wrong for her to have spent that time there? _____

_____ .

d. We must remember there are different seasons in our lives and let God _____

_____ .

e. Why must we stop trying to find some "it" that is never going to change? _____

_____ .

    f. It is much easier to cast our care when we know that _____

        _____.

    g. We need to be careful not to become too attached to anybody or anything in this life more than we are to_____

        _____.

10.   Read Mark 14:3; Hebrews 13:8

    a. Based on the verse in Mark 14:3, why should we not be afraid of brokenness? _____

        _____

        _____.

    b. The perfume of the Holy Spirit is within us, but what has to be done for that sweet fragrance to be released? _____

        _____

        _____.

    c. To fully release the power of the Holy Spirit within us, what must we do? What must we learn?_____

        _____

        _____

        _____

        _____

        _____.

    d. In ancient times, whenever a Roman general returned victoriously from war, why was a slave stationed to ride in a chariot alongside the hero's chariot and given the job of constantly whispering in the hero's ear, "Look behind you," or "Remember that you are mortal"?[1] _____

_____
_____.

e. That is what God does to us. Explain. _____
_____
_____
_____
_____
_____.

f. If we are ever going to have stability in our lives, what must
we do? What must we recall? _____
_____
_____
_____
_____
_____.

g. Why must we put our hope not on the things of this world,
but on the Lord? _____
_____
_____
_____.

11. Read Philippians 4:11-13; Romans 12:3; review Proverbs 16:18

a. Stability is_____.

b. What does it mean to grow up in God? _____
_____
_____
_____

_____

_____.

c. Why was Paul emotionally and spiritually mature? _____

_____

_____

_____.

d. In verse 12 of Philippians chapter 4, what did Paul say on this subject? _____

_____

_____.

e. According to the author, the Lord showed her what would happen if we never had to wait for anything, if everything always went just as we wanted it to, when we wanted it to. Explain. _____

_____

_____

_____

_____

_____.

f. Based on Romans 12:3 and Proverbs 16:18, what must we be on our guard against? _____.

g. God wants to keep His people in balance. He wants to bless us and be good to us. He wants to use us as His vessels through which His Holy Spirit can work. But in order to do that, what must He teach us? _____

_____

_____.

h. Why does God allow us to enjoy wonderful blessings for a time, and then suddenly experience a series of setbacks?

_____

_____

_____.

i. What does God know will happen if we have too many blessings? _____

_____.

j. What does He also know will happen if we have too many bad times? _____

_____.

k. That's why it is so important to remember that whatever comes our way, _____.

l. That's why we must learn to cast it all upon the Lord, knowing that _____

_____.

12. Read Psalm 23:4; Isaiah 43:2; Daniel 3; Daniel 6; review Psalm 91:15

a. In Psalm 23:4, the psalmist David said he _____

_____ the valley of the

shadow of death.

b. That's what we must do. In all the situations and circumstances of this life, what must we remember? _____

_____
_____
_____.

c. What must we be aware of?_____
_____.

d. When the devil tries to whisper to us, "Things will never change, everything will be the same forever; you are trapped!" we should say to him _____
_____
_____
_____!

e. What has the Lord promised us in Isaiah 43:2?_____
_____
_____
_____
_____
_____.

f. What happened when the three Hebrew children were cast into the fiery furnace by King Nebuchadnezzar?_____
_____
_____.

g. What happened when Daniel was thrown into the lions' den?
_____
_____.

h. As we have seen, what does the Lord promise in Psalm 91:15?

_____

_____

_____.

13. Review 2 Corinthians 3:18

a. What is one thing the devil wants us to believe about ourselves? _____.

b. But what does the Bible tell us in the *King James Version* of
this verse? _____

_____

_____

_____.

c. The Greek word translated "transfigured" or "changed" in
this verse is *metamorphoo,* meaning "to transform."[2] It is from
this Greek word we get our English word *metamorphosis,*
which means_____

_____

_____

_____

_____.

d. How does that relate to us spiritually? _____

_____

_____

_____.

e. What should we say to the devil when he tries to tell us we are the same old worm we used to be? _____

_____

_____

_____

_____

_____

_____!

f. Like the caterpillar and the butterfly, what would happen to us if we didn't struggle through some things? _____

_____

_____.

g. God often works through struggle. But He also sometimes works through _____.

14. Read Malachi 3:1; 1 Corinthians 15:51,52; Acts 2:1,2; Acts 9; 16:26-34

a. We all like "suddenlies." What does the Bible promise us as we draw closer to the end times? _____

_____.

b. According to 1 Corinthians 15:51,52, when Jesus comes back to this earth to take us to Himself, we will be changed or transformed_____

_____

_____.

c. Why do we not have to be discouraged in our walk with God?

_____

_____
_____
_____
_____
_____
_____.

d. God is even now in the process of _____
_____, and whatever
_____
He will one day do _____.

e. Just as God worked among the disciples in Acts 2:1,2, how does He work among us today? _____.

f. In the story of the young woman who was filled with the Holy Spirit in one of the author's services, she wrote of how God had suddenly showed up in her life and now He was at work day by day, changing her from glory to glory. That's the way God works — sometimes_____ and sometimes_____, sometimes _____and sometimes
_____
_____.

g. In Acts 9, we read about the conversion of Paul on the road to Damascus. What does the account tell us? _____
_____
_____
_____

_____

_____.

h. From this incident, what should we remember to keep from getting discouraged when we pray for others who are not believers or are not living their faith, and we see no evident change in their attitude or behavior? _____

_____

_____.

i. Why should we never get tired of praying for our loved ones?

_____

_____

_____

_____.

j. As we see in Acts 16:26, how does God work? _____

_____.

k. Just as God moved in the lives of all these people in this passage, He is moving in your life right now. As we have seen, how may He be moving? _____

_____

_____.

l. Whatever may be going on in your life at the moment — good or bad — what should you do?_____

_____

_____.

Retiring From Self-Care

Chapter
9

---

1. Read Acts 16:31

   a. Based on this verse, what does salvation really mean? _____

   _____

   _____

   _____

   _____.

   b. God wants to take care of us. He can do a much better job of that if we will avoid a problem called independence, which is really_____.

   c. Explain the author's statement, "The desire to take care of ourselves is based on fear." _____

   _____

   _____

   _____

   _____

   _____.

   d. The root problem of independence is _____

   _____

   _____.

   e. We love to have a back-up plan. We may pray and ask God to get involved in our lives, but if He is the least bit slow in responding (at least, to our way of thinking), we are quick to take control back into our own hands. When we do that, what do we fail to realize? _____

_____

_____.

2. Read Jeremiah 29:11; John 15:5

   a. It sometimes seems that God refuses to help us when we are faced with a problem. Yet, although He will not help us to meet our own need, He will help us meet someone else's need. What is the reason this happens? _____

_____

_____

_____

_____

_____

_____.

   b. Why do we sometimes have to lay down our plan? _____

_____.

   c. Although it is wise to plan our work and work our plan, what must we not do? _____

_____

_____

_____.

   d. What point was God trying to make in the story of the woman at the gas station who had such an excessive, elaborate plan about how she was going to pay for her gas that her plan was confusing? _____

_____
_____.

e. God does not want us to be independent or codependent. He wants us to be dependent upon Him. Why? _____

_____
_____.

f. What valuable lesson does the woman's testimony contain of which we all need to continually remind ourselves? _____

_____
_____
_____
_____.

3. Read John 5:30

a. Jesus did not ask Himself what to do, He_____
_____. Instead of following His own will, He followed_____
_____. When He made a decision, it was right because_____
_____
_____.

b. What example did Jesus make clear that we would do well to follow?_____
_____.

c. Sometimes rather than deciding the will of God and then being obedient to it, what do we do instead?_____
_____.

d. Jesus said He had no desire to do what was pleasing to Himself. His aim and purpose were _____ _____.

e. What did He say to the people of His day? _____

_____

_____

_____

_____

_____.

f. Jesus did not have a problem with independence, and neither should we. Why? What should we realize? _____

_____

_____

_____

_____.

4. Read 1 Corinthians 13:11

a. In describing her son Danny as a teenager, the author says that like many adolescents, he was self-centered. His every thought, word, and deed had to do with himself and what would bless him and make him happy, when God is the One Who _____

_____

_____

_____.

b. How are immature Christians like young children or teenagers? _____

_____
_____.

   c. If we want to grow up in the Lord, what must we learn? ___

_____
_____.

   d. What must we be determined not to do? _____

_____
_____
_____.

   e. Instead, what must we do? _____

_____
_____
_____.

5.   Read Proverbs 3:5-7; Isaiah 30:21; 2 Chronicles 20:12

   a. Does the passage in Proverbs 3:5-7 mean that we have to seek a divine word from God about every minute decision we make in the course of our daily lives? _____

_____.

   b. How does God put wisdom into us and for what reason? ___

_____
_____.

   c. But the Lord does want us to _____,
_____, and_____Him. He
does want us to be aware of_____
_____ and to walk in _____

_____, _____,

and _____ to Him.

d. God expects us to walk by wisdom, but what does He also expect us to do? _____

_____.

e. Why is acknowledging God in all our ways so important? ___

_____.

f. Based on Isaiah 30:21, what will God do for us if we start to go astray one way or the other? _____

_____

_____.

g. It is_____to God when we go through life planning everything without _____

_____Him or caring what He thinks, yet expecting Him to make everything work out as we envision just because it is _____.

h. Like pride, independence is a sin. Why? _____

_____.

i. Why don't we want anybody to help us? _____

_____

_____.

j. Why does God give each of us only a part of the answer? ___

_____

_____.

k. If we want to do the will of God, we must be willing to____

_____.

l. Usually the stronger our personality, the more weaknesses and inabilities God has to leave in us. Why? _____

_____

_____.

m. In 2 Chronicles 20:12, we read King Jehoshaphat's prayer to the Lord when Judah was faced with an invasion by enemies who were more powerful than they were. What did he acknowledge? _____

_____

_____

_____

_____

_____.

n. What kind of statement is that? _____

_____

_____.

6. Read 1 Corinthians 1:25-29; Zechariah 4:6

a. We must remember it is not our gifts that matter, it is God's

_____.

b. Why does God call people because of their foolishness, ignorance, and weakness rather than their great wisdom, knowledge, or ability? _____

_____.

   c. What two kinds of people does God usually call? _____

     _____

     _____

     _____

     _____

     _____

     _____

     _____

     _____.

   d. Many of us fall into that second category. In that respect, we are no different from _____

     _____.

   e. In the story about the consulting firm, what was the firm basically saying about the people Jesus chose as His disciples?

     _____

     _____

     _____.

   f. Based on Paul's letter to the Corinthians, why does God deliberately choose the nothings of this world? _____

     _____

     _____.

   g. Based on Zechariah 4:6, God takes _____ and adds His _____to them so that they become _____.

h. Since in and of ourselves we are nothing, why must we not try to be independent? _____
_____ .

i. What must we do instead?_____
_____ .

j. What may be the reason we are so independent-minded? __
_____
_____
_____
_____ .

k. If you have been betrayed or mistreated, you may think the only way to protect yourself and assure you are not taken advantage of is by_____
_____ .

l. If so, when God asks you to give up that control to Him, you may find it_____
_____ .

m. What may you also fail to realize is just another form of childish rebellion?_____
_____ .

7. Read Isaiah 30:1,2

a. In this "woe" Scripture passage, upon whom does the Lord pronounce a curse? _____
_____
_____

_____

_____

_____

_____.

b. In this case, to what does fleeing to the "shadow of Egypt" refer? _____

_____

_____.

c. In other words, we are not to trust in ourselves or in others, but only in _____.

d. We are not to make rules and regulations about everything, but, as we have already seen, we are to _____

_____

_____.

e. We are to find our strength in_____, not in _____ or _____, which is what Egypt always represents in Scripture.

8. Read Isaiah 30:3,7

a. According to the author, in this passage, what is the Lord saying to us and why? _____

_____

_____

_____

_____.

b. What does the Lord then say to do before we do anything?

_____

_____

_____

_____

_____

_____.

9. Read Isaiah 30:13,14

a. What happens when we make our own plans or run to other people instead of trusting in the Lord?_____

_____

_____.

b. Then what will happen at a time when we least expect it?__

_____

_____.

c. God does not want us to have weak spots in our lives. What does He want us to do? Why?_____

_____

_____

_____

_____.

d. The more we depend on God, the more_____
_____. But sometimes we
go through a _____ before we
enter into _____.

e. Sometimes before God can promote us, what must He do to us? _____.

f. What did God teach the author that He is teaching all of us today? _____

_____.

10. Read Isaiah 30:15-18

a. According to the author, what is God telling us today? ____

_____

_____

_____

_____.

b. What will happen to us if we don't learn to depend totally upon God? Why? _____

_____

_____

_____.

11. Read John 21:18; 21:15-17; Genesis 22; Hebrews 7:25

a. In the Scripture in John 21:18, the author believes that though God was actually speaking to Peter about the type of death he would experience, the Lord was also letting Peter know something else. What was it? _____

_____

_____

_____

_____

_____.

b. What was another thing that Father God was also letting him know? _____

_____

_____

_____

_____.

c. When we were baby Christians, we did our own thing. We made our own decisions and followed our own course. To demonstrate God's providential care, what did He do for us?

_____

_____.

d. But when we grow up and become mature Christians, we sometimes have to do things we don't particularly want to do in the natural realm, in obedience to God's directions. What does He no longer do for us?_____

_____

_____

_____.

e. For a while, God allows us to "call the shots," so to speak. He lets us do our own thing with His blessing. But what has He been doing to us through that time?_____

_____

_____.

f. At a certain point, God starts "wrestling" with us to call us into submission to His will rather than ours. What has He begun teaching us? _____

_____

_____.

g. In John 21:15-17, what was the reason Jesus had for asking Peter three times, "Simon Peter, do you love Me?" _____

_____

_____.

h. Like the author, when it seems God is asking us to give up the very work He has given us, is He really asking us to give it up? _____

_____

_____

_____.

i. Why does God ask us to do that? _____

_____

_____

_____.

j. How does God test us? _____

_____

_____

_____.

k. What will happen when we get to the place where we can honestly make the kind of commitment the author made, to give God ourselves, our will, and our love and say, "Your will be done, not mine"? _____

_____ .

l. If the Lord loved Peter and knew the plans He had for him,
    plans to bless him and do him good, not to harm him or
    cause him pain, why did He have to deal with him? _____

    _____

    _____ .

m. What did Jesus tell Peter and how does that relate to us?

    _____

    _____ .

12. Read Luke 22:31,32

    a. In this passage, Jesus did not pray that Peter would be deliv-
        ered from testing. He prayed that _____

        _____

        _____

        _____ .

    b. What is Jesus praying for us right now? _____

        _____

        _____

        _____

        _____

        _____ .

    c. It is so important we learn to _____

        _____ and not always
        be looking for somebody else to do it for us.

d. What will happen if we turn our lives over to the Lord totally and completely? _____

_____

_____

_____

_____

_____.

13. Read Luke 10:1-4; Luke 22:35

a. In the passage in Luke 10:1-4, when the Lord sent out the seventy to prepare the way for His arrival, what did He tell them?_____

_____

_____

_____.

b. What is the spiritual principle that the author believes is set forth in this passage? _____

_____

_____

_____

_____

_____

_____

_____.

c. Based on Luke 22:35, if the Lord has sent us out to do His work, it is His responsibility to _____

_____

_____.

d. What has He promised us? _____

_____

_____.

14. Read Matthew 2:1,2,9-11

a. In the Christmas story in this passage, what do we see about Mary and Joseph? _____

_____.

b. If they didn't send out messages asking for gifts, how were their needs met? _____

_____

_____

_____.

c. Explain the basic message of a sermon titled, "The Camels Are Coming" that the author heard preached on this subject in a church in Minnesota. _____

_____

_____

_____

_____

_____.

d. When an avenue in our life is blocked, before we start trying to kick down the door, what do we need to do? Why?_____

_____

_____

_____.

e. Based on Acts 16:7,9, why does God sometimes have to block one avenue? _____

_____.

f. Like the author, rather than getting all riled up and doing something foolish when something we think we need doesn't become ours, what should we do? _____

_____

_____

_____.

g. According to the author, the camels will come for each of us if we will _____

_____.

h. The only way we can expect this kind of provision is by ___

_____

_____

_____.

i. What happens when we begin to believe this? _____

_____

_____

_____

_____

_____
_____.

15. Read 1 Peter 4:19

   a. Based on this passage, in the same way we leave our money with bank officials, trusting them to take care of it for us, what do we need to do each morning in prayer?_____
_____
_____.

   b. When is that especially true?_____
_____
_____
_____.

   c. When we give ourselves up to God, what must we do? Why?
_____
_____
_____
_____.

   d. How did Jesus react when He was abused, reviled, and insulted? _____
_____
_____
_____
_____.

e. As followers of Jesus, our Example, we are called to follow His footsteps. Explain. _____

_____

_____

_____

_____

f. Why do we have no time left to enjoy our lives?_____

_____

_____

_____

_____

g. What will happen if we get so involved in looking out for ourselves? _____

_____

h. Whatever happens to us, however we may be treated or mistreated, what must we do?_____

_____

_____

_____

_____

16. Read Psalm 121:1-8; 17:8

   a. How does the author describe Psalm 121?_____
   _____
   _____
   _____.

   b. According to the author, what should we do with it in the midst of troubled times? _____
   _____.

   c. We have already seen how God has promised to watch over and protect those who take refuge under the shadow of His wings, but how is the pupil of His eye protected, and how does that relate to us? _____
   _____
   _____
   _____
   _____.

17. Read Isaiah 61:6-8; review Hebrews 11:6; read Genesis 15:1

   a. Isaiah 61:6-8 lists some of the rewards God promises His people, and Hebrews 11:6 tells us how we receive those rewards. What does Hebrews 11:6 say of God? _____
   _____
   _____.

   b. So not only is God our Helper and Keeper, He is also the One Who _____ us and _____ us.

c. Based on Genesis 15:1, what is a recompense? _____
_____
_____ .

18. Read Hebrews 10:30

a. What does God mean when He says He is the God of justice?
_____
_____
_____
_____ .

b. As Christians, it is not our job to seek vengeance, but to
_____
_____
_____ .

c. If we will do that, God has promised to _____
_____
_____ .

d. God is not only our Helper and Keeper and the One Who rewards and recompenses us, He is also the Righteous Judge. What does He do? _____
_____
_____ .

e. Why do we need to put the Holy Trinity on our case? _____
_____
_____
_____
_____ .

Prayer for a
Personal Relationship
With the Lord

God wants you to receive His free gift of salvation. Jesus wants to save you and fill you with the Holy Spirit more than anything. If you have never invited Jesus, the Prince of Peace, to be your Lord and Savior, I invite you to do so now. Pray the following prayer, and if you are really sincere about it, you will experience a new life in Christ.

Father,

You loved the world so much, You gave Your only begotten Son to die for our sins so that whoever believes in Him will not perish, but have eternal life.

Your Word says we are saved by grace through faith as a gift from You. There is nothing we can do to earn salvation.

I believe and confess with my mouth that Jesus Christ is Your Son, the Savior of the world. I believe He died on the cross for me and bore all of my sins, paying the price for them. I believe in my heart that You raised Jesus from the dead.

I ask You to forgive my sins. I confess Jesus as my Lord. According to Your Word, I am saved and will spend eternity with You! Thank You, Father. I am so grateful! In Jesus' name, amen.

See John 3:16; Ephesians 2:8,9; Romans 10:9,10; 1 Corinthians 15:3,4; 1 John 1:9; 4:14-16; 5:1,12,13.

Answers

Introduction

1a. Peace.

1b. To be anxious for nothing and to cast our care on Him.

1c. Don't know how to do.

1d. Muddling along in worry or confusion.

1e. Enjoying the abundant life and peace God has for us!

1f. When she began to study the Word of God and apply it to her life.

1g. Live in His peace as a normal condition.

Part 1: Be Anxious for Nothing

Chapter 1

1a. Willed.

1b. That living in turmoil, worry, anxiety, fear, and frustration for a believer is abnormal.

1c. How to receive and live in it.

1d. That as believers, we have a tremendous amount of His protection on us and around us.

1e. God wants to bless us abundantly and is always looking for ways to bless and reach us with His love so that we will be more open to receiving His blessings.

1f. False.

1g. ". . . For I have overcome the world. [I have deprived it of power to harm you and have conquered it for you]."

1h. "Do not let your hearts be troubled. . . ."

1i. Righteousness, peace, and joy in the Holy Spirit.

1j. It is within us.

1k. When we entered into a personal relationship with Jesus.

1l. Joy and peace.

1m. Through believing.

2a. The God of hope will fill us with all joy and peace as we believe, so that we may abound and be overflowing — bubbling over — with hope.

2b. We who truly believe.

2c. A childlike attitude of faith.

2d. Because the basis of their joy has been misplaced.

2e. Our names are enrolled in heaven.

2f. Believing.

2g. They come as a result of building our relationship with the Lord. Because in His presence is fullness of joy; if we have received Jesus as our Savior and Lord, He, the Prince of Peace lives inside us.

2h. We experience peace in the Lord's presence, receiving from Him and acting in response to His direction.

2i. Knowing, believing — trusting in the Lord with simple childlike faith.

Chapter 2

1a. A heaviness.

1b. As "... a state of uneasiness; worry ... Abnormal fear that lacks a specific cause."[1]

1c. (Your answer.)

2a. "Evil forebodings."

2b. "Little foxes, that spoil the vines."

2c. We won't have much peace or joy.

2d. "Stop it!"

2e. We can see that we can control the way we respond to something that might trouble us. We can choose peace or trouble. We can choose to stay calm or to calm down if we start becoming agitated.

2f. For the Word's sake.

2g. "Cheer up!"

2h. Jesus, Who lives inside those of us who believe in Him, has overcome the world.

2i. By letting the Holy Spirit lead you step-by-step on a path that will take you into freedom!

3a. A peaceful spirit that is not anxious or wrought up.

3b. To be tense, tied in a knot, upset and disturbed.

3c. To be worried, disquieted, or distracted.

3d. He wants to keep us from focusing our attention on the good things God has given us. He wants to keep us from enjoying our relationship with the Lord and the abundant life Jesus died to provide for us.

3e. We need to learn to relax, lighten up, and let things go. We need to learn that even if everything does not always work out exactly as we want it to, it will not be the end of the world.

4a. To take thought or being "... apprehensive, or worried about what may happen; concern about a possible future event."[2]

4b. "Anxiety is caused by trying to mentally and emotionally get into things that are not here yet or things that have already been" — mentally leaving where you are and getting into an area of the past or the future.

4c. To be sober-minded, vigilant, and cautious, on our guard against our enemy, the devil, who is out to devour us.

4d. To enjoy the good life God has provided for us through the death and resurrection of His Son Jesus Christ.

4e. "This is the day the Lord has made; I will rejoice and be glad in it."

4f. Laugh. If we would just laugh a little more — "be of good cheer," "cheer up" — we would find that a little bit of laughter makes that load much lighter.

4g. Work on it a little. We need to laugh and have a good time.

5a. To rejoice. Not to fret or have any anxiety about anything but to pray and give thanks to God in everything — not after everything is over.

5b. By learning to enjoy life even in the midst of trying circumstances.

5c. There are many stages we must go through in the course of our spiritual growth.

5d. How to enjoy the glory we are experiencing at each level of our development.

5e. We need to learn to rejoice and be glad in the Lord this day and every day along the way toward our goal.

5f. "He has made me glad; He has made me glad; I will rejoice for He has made me glad."

5g. Presence; presents.

5h. Face.

5i. Find something to be glad about besides our current circumstances.

5j. The devil will see to that because he knows that anxiety in a man's heart weighs it down.

5k. Give that anxiety to the Lord in prayer with thanksgiving, making our requests known to Him. Then the peace that passes all understanding will keep our hearts and minds in Christ Jesus.

6a. Three.

6b. 1. The past and the future. 2. Confrontations and conversations. 3. Duties and obligations of the day.

7a. Mentally leaving where you are and getting into an area of the past or the future.

7b. That God wants us to learn to be "now people."

7c. Learn to live now — mentally as well as physically and spiritually.

7d. Because we are more occupied with the past or the future than we are with the present.

7e. We are to keep a balance in life.

7f. Today.

7g. Because Jesus is always in the present.

7h. We don't need to worry about anything. All we need to do is seek the Kingdom of God, and He will add to us whatever we need, whether it is food or clothing or shelter or spiritual growth.

7i. Because tomorrow will have problems of its own.

7j. Concentrate our full attention on today and stop being so intense and wrought up.

7k. Because it will never come again.

7l. Handle; cast. Because the Lord cares for us.

7m. Learn; prepare; live.

8a. When they went out into the world to preach the Gospel to every creature, as He was commanding them to do, they would run into opposition.

8b. By instructing His disciples not to worry about what to say or even try to figure out or meditate upon it, because when they opened their mouths to speak, it would not be them speaking but the Holy Spirit within them.

8c. You think the outcome of that conversation depends upon you and your ability rather than upon the Holy Spirit and His ability.

8d. We are not trusting in the anointing of God but in ourselves.

8e. We will not do as well as if we were depending completely on God!

8f. Favor. Then we can be confident that whatever the results of our conversation or confrontation, it is the will of God, and it will work out for the best for all concerned.

9a. Martha is upset and distracted because she is overly occupied and too busy, while Mary is happily seated at the feet of Jesus enjoying His presence and fellowship.

9b. That she could not enjoy life because she was too complicated.

9c. She needed to learn to be more like Mary and less like Martha. Instead of worrying and fretting, she needed to learn to simplify her plans, lighten up, and enjoy life!

9d. (Your answers.)

Chapter 3

1a. The arm of the flesh and the arm of the Lord.

1b. One of these is "our deal," the other is "God's deal"; that is, one is based on human ideas and effort, the other is based on God's plan and power. One is of the flesh, the other is of the Spirit.

1c. Maintained; maintained.

1d. When we try to operate in the arm of the flesh we end up frustrated, but when we operate in the arm of the Lord we end up victorious.

1e. It is hard work to carry out the plans and schemes we ourselves have devised. But when God starts something, He carries it through to completion without any struggle on our part.

1f. Often the problem is not the devil but ourselves. We are trying to accomplish our will and plan, not the will and plan of God.

1g. Operating in the arm of the flesh rather than the arm of the Lord.

1h. He will finish it.

2a. The adversary will oppose us.

2b. That greater is He Who is in us than he who is in the world.

2c. Although he may come at us one way, he will have to flee from us seven ways.

2d. Sometimes we spend more time talking about Satan than we do talking about God.

2e. When He appeared on the scene, they either fled in terror or were driven out by Him with a word.

2f. Stand strong in the authority given us by Jesus.

2g. Stay in God's will and plan by operating in the arm of the Lord and not the arm of the flesh.

2h. They try to resist the devil without submitting themselves to God!

2i. A mature individual is patient and waits on the Lord to work out things according to His perfect will and timing. Immature people rush ahead of God and end up frustrated.

2j. She give birth to Ishmaels instead of Isaacs.

3a. That He would bless him and give him an heir from his own body so that his descendants would be as numerous as the stars in the heavens.

3b. A plan to produce an heir for Abraham by having him take her handmaid Hagar as his "secondary wife."

3c. The Lord appeared to Abraham and again promised to bless him and make him the father of many nations. He then went on to bless Sarah and promised to give Abraham a son by her in their old age.

3d. It was through this promised son, Isaac, and not through the natural son, Ishmael. Isaac was God's idea and plan; Ishmael was Sarah's idea and plan. One was the child of promise, the child of the Spirit; the other was the child of human effort, the child of the flesh.

3e. Ishmael caused problems in the household, so Abraham had to send Ishmael and his mother Hagar away.

3f. Because we have produced Ishmaels rather than Isaacs. We are reaping the consequences of trying to carry out our own ideas and plans rather than waiting for God to bring forth His ideas and plans.

3g. We get angry at God because He is not making everything work out as we want it to.

3h. That what is born of the Spirit is spirit, and what is born of the flesh is flesh.

4a. He told us that it is the Spirit Who is important, not the flesh. Because the Spirit gives life while the flesh profits nothing.

4b. The flesh — the selfish, rebellious sin nature within us — has to die.

4c. Within us; the outside.

4d. He described how miserable he was because he failed to practice the good deeds he desired to do, but succeeded in doing the evil deeds he did not want to do.

4e. He cried out, "O unhappy and pitiable and wretched man that I am! Who will release and deliver me from [the shackles of] this body of death?"

4f. All of that is a testing ground, one which we must all go through.

4g. To teach us to deny the flesh and depend on the Spirit in order to build character in us as we go through the hard times and refuse to give up.

4h. If we are committed to doing what God has told us to do.

4i. Instead of getting God's plan and being obedient to Him as He works it out, we try to make up our own plan and get Him to bless it.

4j. We get angry at Him; we get confused and often very negative in our emotions and conversations.

4k. Because He didn't make their plan work. (Your answer.)

4l. We are trying to kick doors open and make our own way.

4m. We should wait on the Lord, believe and trust in Him, and enjoy where we are and what we are doing until He opens the doors for us.

4n. To believe, not to cook up all kinds of plans and schemes to try to make things happen.

4o. Leading; "trying."

4p. The discovery that we are all wrong sometimes.

4q. We try to live by the flesh, by works, rather than by the Spirit.

5a. The covenant of works and the covenant of grace.

5b. On man's doing everything on his own, struggling, striving, and laboring to be acceptable to God.

5c. It steals joy and peace.

5d. It is based not on what man can do, but on what Christ has already done.

5e. It takes the pressure off of us to perform.

5f. One brings bondage; the other brings liberty.

5g. Believe; believe; act on what God tells us to do.

5h. They have no hope, peace, or joy.

5i. Be bubbling over with joy. We will also see much more positive results in our lives.

6a. Those who do not labor to bring forth their own results but who depend entirely upon the grace of God will enjoy more results than those who wear themselves out trying to produce by their own efforts.

6b. Because God's people are trying to do with the arm of flesh what can only be done by the arm of the Lord.

6c. Because the writers of these Scriptures are talking about spiritual, not natural, children.

6d. It means that she has given up trying to give birth the natural way. Instead, she has learned to put her faith and trust in God to give birth spiritually. She has ceased from her labor and has entered the rest of God.

6e. They end up having more children — enjoying more and better results — than those who try to produce by their own works.

7a. False.

7b. That we can have inexpressible, glorious, triumphant, heavenly joy right in the very midst of our trials and temptations.

7c. We need to ask why not.

7d. Something can be available to us yet never be of any benefit to us because we never avail ourselves of it.

7e. We will live in the frustration of works.

7f. "Works of the flesh."

7g. We only benefit from the blessings of the covenant of grace by living under grace. As long as we live under works, we will be frustrated and depressed because we are trying to do God's job.

7h. To be our Helper in life.

7i. Because they don't want any help. They want to do everything for themselves.

7j. By simply asking for it.

7k. Because asking for help is an acknowledgment that we are not able to do everything for ourselves.

8a. If we are full of pride and doing things our own way without listening to Him, we will end up in situations that will result in anxiety and stress.

8b. He is trying to set us up for a blessing. Or He may be trying to protect us from something we don't know about.

8c. Because it will keep us from experiencing peace and joy in this life.

8d. To overcome all of our evil tendencies.

8e. Exactly what Peter said in his first letter to the believers: ". . . God sets Himself against the proud and haughty, but gives grace [continually] to the lowly (those who are humble enough to receive it)."

8f. "Humble yourselves [feeling very insignificant] in the presence of the Lord, and He will exalt you [He will lift you up and make your lives significant]."

8g. By humbling ourselves before Him, casting all our cares upon Him, and trusting Him to take care of them as He has promised in His Word.

8h. Because they think they can handle everything for themselves.

8i. Because they know they can't handle everything — only God can.

9a. "Except the Lord builds the house, they labor in vain who build it. . . ."

9b. Us.

9c. We are.

9d. Building; Chief Cornerstone.

9e. One brick at a time, day by day, from glory to glory.

9f. The difference between works and faith.

10a. Having begun our new lives in Christ by dependence on the Spirit, are we now trying to live them in the flesh?

10b. By grace (God's unmerited favor) through faith, and not by works of the flesh.

10c. We are still in no condition to help ourselves!

10d. (Your answer.)

10e. By submitting ourselves to God and letting Him do the work in us that needs to be done.

10f. Only the Spirit.

11a. ". . . the perfecting and the full equipping of the saints (His consecrated people), [that they should do] the work of ministering toward building up Christ's body (the church). . . ."

11b. "... really mature manhood. ...."

11c. "... (the completeness of personality which is nothing less than the standard height of Christ's own perfection), the measure of the stature of the fullness of the Christ and the completeness found in Him."

11d. (Your answer.)

11e. To mature and be Christlike in our attitude and behavior, to know Jesus and the power of His resurrection, to measure up to His stature and operate in the fruit of His Spirit.

11f. Be willing to be changed and humbly submit ourselves to the Lord, allowing Him to build us into the people He wants us to be.

11g. Through faith.

12a. The leaning of the entire human personality on God in absolute trust and confidence in His power, wisdom, and goodness.

12b. To abide in the Lord, to lean on Him totally and completely, to put our trust and confidence in Him.

12c. Confess those sins. We get into agreement with God about them.

12d. Acknowledge our inability to do anything about our sins. The more we try to change ourselves, the worse we get.

12e. Believe.

12f. Cleave to, trust in, rely on, and have faith in Him and His Son Jesus Christ.

12g. Anxious or worried. Build ourselves; build us and equip us.

13a. God; Jesus.

13b. Build us and equip us.

13c. "It was God Who started this work in you, and it is God Who will finish it!"

13d. That means we should leave God alone to do His work.

13e. We are to confess our sins and failures to the Lord, confident that He will forgive us of those sins and failures and cleanse us from all unrighteousness, as He has promised in His Word.

13f. That takes the pressure off of us, which relieves us of the worry and anxiety we feel so often as we try to perfect ourselves.

14a. Stay away from wrong behavior and allow the Lord of peace Himself to sanctify us, preserve us, complete us, hallow us, and keep us.

14b. They are our call from God to a certain kind of holy living. They are also our assurance that it is not we who bring about this holy life, but God Himself, Who can be trusted utterly to do the work in and for us.

14c. Our part is to believe. Our work is to trust the Lord. His requirement is that we let go and let God.

15a. To build us.

15b. Ourselves.

15c. Our ministry.

15d. Our reputation.

16a. The choice between pleasing men and pleasing God.

16b. Our Lord did not set out to make a name for Himself, and neither should we.

16c. It will cause us to live in fear of man rather than in fear of God. We will try to win favor with people rather than with the Lord.

16d. ". . . stand fast then, and do not be hampered and held ensnared and submit again to a yoke of slavery [which you have once put off]."

16e. The threat of rejection.

16f. Are we going to go on trying to build ourselves, our ministries, and our reputations, or are we willing to give up all our human efforts and simply trust God? Are we ready to stop operating in the arm of the flesh and start operating in the arm of the Lord?

Chapter 4

1a. While the arm of the flesh is based on the covenant of works, the arm of the Lord is based on the covenant of grace.

1b. The first depends upon law, the second depends upon faith.

1c. Under the first covenant we wear ourselves out trying to make things happen on our own. Under the second covenant we enter into the rest of God and depend upon Him to do for us what we cannot do for ourselves.

1d. To present our bodies as a living sacrifice, holy and well pleasing to God, which is our reasonable service and spiritual worship.

1e. 1) Willing, 2) yielded, and 3) empty.

1f. We must be willing for God to use us as He sees fit. We must be willing to follow His plans rather than our own. We must be empty of ourselves.

1g. Give up all our human efforts to build ourselves, our ministries, and our careers and allow the Lord to build them for us according to His will and plan for us. Learn to be satisfied where we are and with what we are doing. Quit worrying and fretting and simply allow the Lord to do the work in us and through us that He knows needs to be done.

1h. Quit looking to the arm of the flesh and start looking to the arm of the Lord.

2a. The mistake he made was telling that dream, because it was one of the things that made his brothers so hateful, envious, and angry that they tried to get rid of him by selling him into slavery.

2b. Joseph was a little overly exuberant.

2c. When God reveals to us His dream and vision for our life, we share it with others who are not as thrilled about it as we are and who may even cause us problems, just as Joseph's brothers did for him.

2d. Joseph ended up alone in a prison cell in Egypt far from home and family with no one to turn to but the Lord.

2e. Periods in which we have to stand alone.

2f. We are forced to place our entire faith and trust in God.

2g. The arm of the Lord; the arm of the flesh.

2h. We may follow the advice people give us instead of seeking God's direction.

2i. Most birds fly in flocks, but eagles fly alone.

2j. We must decide whether we want to fly along as one of the many birds in a flock or be an eagle.

2k. Learn to fly alone.

2l. But God was with him.

3a. He built his reputation and career. He put him in the right place at the right time. He gave him favor with the right people and promoted him when the time was right.

3b. When God is ready to move in our lives, He will give us favor and promotion.

3c. ". . . If God is for us, who [can be] against us? [Who can be our foe, if God is on our side?]"

3d. People who are willing, yielded, and empty.

3e. Let God build you, your ministry, and your reputation and career. When the time is right, He will deliver you just as He delivered Joseph. Then you will see the fulfillment of your dream, just as Joseph did.

4a. Regardless of what people may have tried to do to us, God can take it and turn it for good.

4b. Meant good to him.

4c. He knew it didn't matter who was against him, because God was for him and would eventually work out everything for the best for all concerned. He knew that whatever happened, God was on his side.

4d. He let God build his life, his reputation, and his career.

5a. God went to work on her and began to change her.

5b. He will do the same for you, if you will keep your eyes on Him and not on yourself.

6a. Either we will spend our lives trying to take care of ourselves or we will let go and let God take care of us as we put our faith and trust in Him.

6b. Because all flesh is as frail as grass. Like the flowers of the field, it is here today and gone tomorrow.

6c. We must humble ourselves under His mighty hand and wait upon Him to exalt us in His good time.

7a. It means to submit all our plans to Him to work them out according to His will and desire for us.

7b. What He wants is for us to come to know Him in the power of His resurrection and to behold Him in all His beauty and glory.

7c. To dwell in God's presence. Because only there can we experience the fullness of joy.

7d. His hand is always open to us.

7e. To grow up in all things unto the stature of His Son Jesus Christ.

7f. Should; want; should.

8a. ". . . If the Lord is willing, we shall live and we shall do this or that [thing]."

8b. What God wants.

8c. Better for us in the long run.

8d. When we do that, we are showing Him disrespect by not acknowledging Him in our plans.

8e. It says, "Pride goes before destruction, and a haughty spirit before a fall."

8f. Humility.

8g. So that He may exalt us in due time.

8h. By waiting on the Lord, refusing to move in the energy of the flesh.

8i. Acknowledge; honors; our heart's desire!

8j. Attitude.

9a. Knowing who we are in Jesus.

9b. To recognize we are empty.

9c. The power of God that is resident there to flow out of us.

9d. Nothing.

9e. Only the value the Lord assigns to us because of the blood of His Son Jesus Christ.

9f. What is born of flesh is flesh, and it profits us nothing.

9g. He said, ". . . the life I now live in the body I live by faith in (by adherence to and reliance on and complete trust in) the Son of God. . . ."

9h. The Lord ". . . will continue until the day of Jesus Christ [right up to the time of His return], developing [that good work] and perfecting and bringing it to full completion . . . ."

9i. We will all eventually be like the woman in 2 Kings 4:1-7 — empty of ourselves and ready to be used by God to fill other empty people.

9j. We must realize and acknowledge what we cannot do. We must get our eyes off of ourselves and our limited ability, and totally onto Him and His infinite power.

10a. 1) "We have no might to stand against this great company that is coming against us," 2) "We do not know what to do," and 3) "But our eyes are on You."

10b. When we reach the place of being able to make these three statements to the Lord in total honesty and complete dependence upon Him.

10c. The answer may be that we are still too full of ourselves.

10d. We won't let go of it.

11a. 1) Acknowledge we have no power to save ourselves, 2) admit we do not know what to do about our situation, and 3) turn our eyes upon the Lord, placing our faith and trust in Him to deliver us.

11b. Once we stop looking to the arm of flesh for our solution.

11c. "Be still."

11d. "Let God arise and His enemies be scattered!"

11e. That when He rises up, every knee shall bow and every tongue shall confess that Jesus Christ is Lord, to the glory of God the Father.

11f. He told them to take up their positions, stand still, and see the deliverance of the Lord.

11g. Because God was with them.

11h. All the people bowed their faces to the ground and worshipped the Lord.

11i. Planning; scheming; trying to tell God what He needs to do.

11j. Resists; gives grace.

12a. "God helps those who help themselves"; unscriptural.

12b. Cannot help themselves; depend not upon our own efforts, plans, and schemes to get us through this life and solve all our problems.

12c. This statement tends to make people feel as though they need to do all they possibly can for themselves before ever asking God to help.

12d. Believe that lie and spend our lives in frustration trying to take care of ourselves rather than leaning on God.

12e. Those who know they cannot help themselves, those who, like King Jehoshaphat and the people of Judah, realize that they are totally dependent upon Him for their deliverance.

13a. The everlasting arms of the Lord coming down and lifting us up.

13b. We should experience the manifest presence of God with us as we make the conscious decision to no longer lean on the arm of the flesh, but on the arm of the Lord.

14a. Looking to the Lord and trusting in His wisdom, strength, and power.

14b. The One Who is with us is greater than all those who oppose us.

14c. They are like a plant in the desert that is dry and destitute. They will not see any good come.

14d. They are like a tree planted by a river. They do not cease to produce fruit even in the midst of a drought. No matter what comes, they will flourish and ". . . shall not be anxious and full of care. . . ."

14e. We are not to lean on ourselves or on other people, but on God.

14f. Love; trust.

15a. Because He knew what was in human nature.

15b. He just didn't open Himself up to them and give Himself to them in the same way He trusted God and opened Himself up to His heavenly Father.

15c. Because we form relationships with people we should not be involved with. We become too familiar with them, start depending upon then idolizing them, and looking to them when we should be looking to God.

15d. It happens because we are not perfect.

15e. The strong arm of the Lord.

15f. We always end up disappointed and hurt.

Chapter 5

1a. We ". . . do enter that [God's] rest. . . ."

1b. Simply by refusing to become upset.

1c. We are in this world, but not of it.

1d. Hard times: "hard to deal with and hard to bear."

1e. The times we are living in today and one action we are to take.

1f. ". . . out of them all the Lord delivered me."

1g. What our response to living in this kind of atmosphere and situation should be.

1h. Instead of stopping to check with their heart to see if it is right, they find someone who teaches what they want to hear and go there.

1i. Truth; teaching; counsel.

1j. "I am to be calm, cool, and collected"!

1k. "A wild spirit."

1l. Make sure we are acting in obedience to the leading of the Lord and not just reacting out of emotion.

1m. That works not energized by God are "dead works" and do not produce any good result.

2a. We are to take a stand, after having done all in our power that God has led us to do.

2b. What we do to overcome one crisis may not be what we are to do to handle the next crisis that arises.

2c. Because the solution to the problem is not in the procedure, it is in the power — which God gives us to accomplish what He directs us to do.

2d. Different; different; different.

2e. The power of God flowing through Jesus.

2f. Release the faith within each person to whom He ministered.

2g. Faith.

3a. ". . . because it was not mixed with faith (with the leaning of the entire personality on God in absolute trust and confidence in His power, wisdom, and goodness) by those who heard it. . . ."

3b. Because if we are not abiding in His rest, we are not operating in true faith.

3c. That without faith it is impossible to please God.

3d. Place. Secret place. The presence of the Lord.

3e. Because we know that in the presence of the Lord there is joy, peace, and rest.

4a. He assured Moses His presence would be with him and give him rest.

4b. All that Moses needed.

4c. His presence will be with us wherever He sends us and in whatever He gives us to do.

4d. Stay relaxed and trust God to show us what to do.

4e. If it was God Who ruined our plan, we had the wrong plan to begin with. If it was the devil who ruined our plan, the Lord will give us another plan, one that will be ten times better than the one that failed.

4f. We start rebuking the devil.

4g. We talk to the wrong person.

4h. Learn to turn to the Lord and say, "Father, You are my Refuge and my Fortress, my God; on You I lean and rely, and in You I confidently trust."

5a. Of the person who dwells in the secret place of the Most High, who claims the Lord as his Refuge and Fortress, and who leans, relies, and confidently trusts in Him.

5b. All the promises of God's provision and protection.

5c. Basically, they are that we stay in rest.

5d. The "wild spirit" that so often motivates us to lose our self-control so that we say and do things that cause pain and problems for us as well as for others.

5e. Promises; presence; peace.

6a. His peace.

6b. ". . . Peace to you!"

6c. To live in peace.

6d. "Stop allowing yourselves to be anxious, worried, and upset."

6e. We need to hope in God and wait expectantly for Him, Who is our Help and our God.

6f. Peace; place.

7a. Seated at the right hand of God the Father in heavenly places.

7b. Seated also.

8a. The Word of God; the Upholder, Sustainer, and Redeemer of the universe; at the right hand of God on high.

8b. God; footstool.

9a. By speaking forth the Word of God in faith.

9b. That we are not the ones who exercise ultimate power and authority over the enemy.

9c. It means that although Jesus has given us power and authority over the devil and his demons on this earth, in the end it is God Himself Who is ultimately going to take away from Satan every bit of his power and send him to his final place of eternal punishment.

10a. He is waiting ". . . until His enemies should be made a stool beneath His feet."

10b. Because under the covenant of works the people were not allowed to sit down and rest.

10c. After Jesus had gone into the true Holy of Holies and sprinkled His own blood on the heavenly altar.

10d. He had to be ministering to the Lord.

10e.   He said to Him, "Well done. Your work is finished. Sit here at My right hand until I make your enemies Your footstool."

10f.   He wants us to know we are seated at His right hand with His Son Jesus Christ.

10g.   We can enter into His throne room and find rest for our souls.

11a.   God wants us not only to enter into His rest in our body, He also wants us to enter into His rest in our soul.

11b.   It means finding freedom from mental activity. It means not having to constantly try to figure out what we should do about everything in our life. It means not having to live in torment of reasoning, always trying to come up with an answer we don't have. We don't have to worry; instead we can remain calm in a place of quiet peace and rest.

11c.   Speak to our raging soul and tortured mind just as Jesus spoke to the wind and waves by simply saying: "Peace, be still."

11d.   We are walking in authority over Satan.

12a.   By our ". . . steadfastness and patient endurance. . . ."

12b.   Let our mind and emotions get the best of us, especially when it involves things we have no control over.

12c.   Do the rest.

12d.   What God protected us from.

12e.   Learn to possess our souls and not give the devil a foothold in our lives.

13a.   Our soul rises up and causes strife.

13b.   Because many times the thing we think we don't want is the best thing for us.

13c.   We need to learn to adapt, to let things go, to quit allowing our souls to rule our lives. We need to learn to walk by the Spirit and not by the flesh.

13d.   We throw open the door for the devil. We give him an opportunity to come in and wreak havoc.

13e.   Choose to honor Him by staying in peace.

13f.   No. It just means we need to manage our feelings and not let them manage us.

14a.   Our constancy and fearlessness.

14b.   Our constancy and fearlessness in the face of his onset.

14c.   Often it is because God is waiting to see if we really trust Him or not.

14d.   Think we have to be up and running around doing something, like the Old Testament priests in the Holy of Holies.

14e.   "I'm going to stay seated in Christ and enjoy the rest of the Lord while He handles this situation and uses it to bless me."

15a.	To build our spiritual character as well as our spiritual power.

15b.	To overcome every problem of life by rebuking the devil.

15c.	He is working to get us to the point where, no matter what is going on around us, we remain the same, rooted and grounded in Christ and His love, standing firm on the Rock of our salvation.

15d.	So He can give us power to keep ourselves calm in the days of adversity.

15e.	Wait patiently and confidently for our promised deliverance and salvation, and for the impending destruction of all our enemies.

15f.	Anxious for nothing.

Part 2: Cast All Your Care

Introduction

1a.	Because He cares for us.

1b.	God wants to take care of us.

1c.	We must stop taking the care upon ourselves and start casting it upon Him.

1d.	He will give us something in return.

2a.	To give us several positive things in exchange for the negative things in our lives.

2b.	To give us beauty for ashes.

2c.	He cannot give us His beauty.

2d.	Be willing to give Him the messes in our lives.

2e.	Blessings; messes.

3a.	Not to be anxious about anything but to turn from the arm of the flesh and depend upon the arm of the Lord as we remain calm — quietly and confidently seated with Christ in heavenly places.

3b.	Several issues relating to our care.

Chapter 6

1a.	Many of the blessings offered us by the Lord in exchange for our "messes."

1b.	Meet the conditions of the first two verses, which is that we dwell in the secret place of the Most High, remaining stable and fixed under the shadow of the Almighty.

1c.	First, we must *dwell,* which means "to remain . . . to settle . . . continue . . . sit (-down)."[1]

1d.	Second, we must dwell in the "secret place" of the Most High, meaning a hiding place, a place of protection, a place with a covering over it so we will be kept safe from all our enemies.

1e. Third, we must remain under the "shadow" of the Almighty, meaning we must make the Lord our Refuge and our Fortress, leaning and relying on Him and confidently trusting in Him.

2.   He will deliver us, cover us, keep us from fear and terror, and protect us against evil plots and slander so that we have no fear of pestilence, destruction, or sudden death, even though others may be falling from these things all around us.

3a. God promises angelic protection and deliverance to those who are serving Him and walking in obedience to Him.

3b. In a position of power and authority over Satan and his demons and devices.

3c. Favor; influence.

3d. It means we are protected from what Satan ultimately has planned for us as long as we keep our trust in God and say the right things of Him.

3e. We must learn it is a process.

3f. The Lord promises us that when we call upon Him, He will answer us and be with us in our troubles and will strengthen us and accompany us through them to victory, deliverance, and honor.

3g. God is with us in our trials and troubles, then He begins to deliver us out of them, and afterwards He honors us.

4a. Instead of getting all anxious and upset and weeping and wailing, go into the secret place of the Lord and lift up shouts of joy while the devil is trying to destroy us. Find refuge and remain stable and fixed under the shadow of the Almighty.

4b. He fights our battles.

5a. A shadow is a shade, a protection from the heat or the sun. It is also a border between light and dark.

5b. There are definite borders or limits within which we must stay if we are to remain under the shadow of God's wings — that is, under His protection against the world or the devil.

5c. We will be much more comfortable and much better protected against danger than when we choose to walk out from under those wings.

5d. Take up permanent residence there.

5e. Trust and confidence.

5f. He will keep us under the shadow of His wings and protect us from all danger and harm.

6a. "Pray and don't worry."

6b. Because prayer is supposed to be the way we cast our care upon the Lord.

6c. Turn and give that care to God.

6d. In prayer. That's what prayer is, our acknowledgment to the Lord that we cannot carry our burden of care, so we lay it all on Him.

6e. We are mixing a positive and a negative. The two cancel each other out so that we end up right back where we started — at zero.

6f. They cancel out their positive prayer power by giving in to the negative power of worry.

6g. As long as we are worrying, we are not trusting God. It is only by trusting, by having faith and confidence in the Lord, that we are able to enter into His rest and enjoy the peace that transcends all understanding.

7a. Believing. Because the fruit of believing is rest.

7b. We have entered into His rest.

7c. Abiding in the perfect peace of His holy presence.

8a. Experience with God.

8b. Years of experience.

8c. The patience, endurance, and character that will eventually produce the habit of joyful and confident hope.

8d. Experience; strength. Stronger.

8e. Sooner or later we will be more than the devil can handle.

8f. Spiritual maturity.

8g. In secret. Privately.

8h. The intended work never gets accomplished.

8i. He works them out for our good.

9a. That He would be silent and submissive, a sign of His inner strength and stability.

9b. We get to know the Lord and, like the apostle Paul, learn to be quiet and confident in whatever circumstances we may find ourselves.

10a. The ability to be content in whatever state he found himself.

10b. He knew how to cast his cares upon the Lord and remain in the secret place under the shadow of His wings.

10c. He knew how to live day by day without being disturbed or disquieted.

10d. He said it was something he had learned to do — and that takes time and experience.

10e. If we keep following the Lord, being faithful and obedient to Him regardless of what may happen to us.

11a. He will continually tempt us to "take the road of worry" so he can lead us off into destruction.

11b. We can remain within the boundaries of God's guidance and protection.

11c. Trust the Lord to lead us in the way we should go and get us safely to our final destination.

11d. When we begin to lose our peace.

11e. Be sensitive to our lack of peace and find the reason for it so we can correct the problem and move back into the way of the Lord.

11f. To trust in the Lord not just with our heart, but with our heart and our mind.

11g. Entire human personality; trust; confidence.

11h. He means totally, completely. He means we are to trust Him mentally and emotionally as well as spiritually.

11i. Being in constant turmoil and confusion.

12a. About the futility of worry and anxiety.

12b. Read these verses out loud.

12c. To stop being perpetually uneasy, worried, and anxious.

12d. Because when we do that we are not only harming ourselves, we are also being disobedient to God.

12e. Just as God feeds the birds and animals and even clothes the grass and flowers of the field, so He will feed and clothe those of us who put our faith and trust in Him.

12f. Our heavenly Father knows all the things we have need of and that He has promised to provide them for us.

12g. We are to seek first God's Kingdom and His righteousness, and then all these other things will be given to us as well.

12h. Simply because we have the wrong priorities. We are seeking security in the things of this world rather than in the Creator of this world.

12i. He has promised to provide all the answers we need.

12j. We are told to seek God and His righteousness, trusting Him to provide all these other things He knows we need in accordance with His divine plan and timing.

13a. That he might dwell in the presence of the Lord and behold His beauty all the days of his life.

13b. If we seek to dwell in the secret place of the Most High, leaning and relying on Him in confidence and trust, He will add to us all the blessings He has promised in the rest of that psalm.

13c. We are not to seek after the things of this life, but to seek first God's Kingdom and His righteousness.

13d. We are not to be worried or anxious about tomorrow, because tomorrow will have worries and anxieties of its own; it is enough for us to deal with each day's cares as they arise.

13e. How we are to deal with each day's cares — by casting them all on the Lord Who cares for us affectionately and cares about us watchfully.

13f. We are told to fret not ourselves and to avoid anxious thoughts, which can quickly become irritating. Instead, we are to place our faith and confidence in the Lord, Who is our Refuge and our Fortress.

14a. Not God plus something else, but God only.

14b. We should do as David did and climb up on the rock that is higher than we are.

14c. A castle, a fort, a defense, a place into which we go when we are being hunted or attacked. It is not a hiding place in which our enemy cannot find us. It is a place of protection in which we can see and be seen but cannot be reached because we are safe in God's protection.

14d. His High Tower — another lofty and inaccessible place — and his Shield and Buckler — which are part of the protective armor that surrounds the believer.

14e. He is not just above us and around us, He is even underneath us.

14f. He is holding us up by His powerful right hand and is surrounding us as the mountains surround the holy city of Jerusalem.

14g. For; over; with; in.

14h. He watches over us and keeps us so we can find rest and peace under the shadow of His wings as we cast all our care upon Him.

Chapter 7

1a. Care; responsibility.

1b. We do just the opposite; we cast our responsibility, but keep our care.

1c. Casting our care; being passive.

1d. To believe.

1e. Because if God has told us something, we should have no problem believing it and doing what He says for us to do.

1f. To cast all of our care upon Him, which itself can be something of a violent matter.

2a. Because it refers to throwing, hurling, arising, sending, striking, thrusting, driving out, or expelling — all rather forceful terms.[1]

2b. He said that since the days of John the Baptist, the Kingdom of God has endured violent assault, and violent men have seized it by force.

2c. We are going to have to get violent — spiritually violent — about casting our care upon the Lord and abiding in the secret place of the Most High, under the shadow of the Almighty.

2d. In our absolute refusal to live any longer under guilt and condemnation, which can actually be worry about past mistakes.

2e. He pressed on to take hold of those things for which Christ Jesus had laid hold on him.

2f. Rise up against the principalities, powers, and wickedness in high places; all the blessings bought for us by Jesus Christ.

2g. The devil and his demons.

2h. We can resist and resist Satan and the guilt, condemnation, worry, and anxiety he tries to place on us, until we get so fed up we react with a holy anger.

2i. We can stop and violently take back what Satan is trying to take from us by saying, "No! I will not carry that care. I am casting it upon the Lord!"

2j. We need to engage in some holy violence. When we feel the devil starting to lay any kind of guilt, condemnation, and care upon us, we need to take it and cast it upon the Lord.

2k. We need to cast them upon the Lord.

2l. "'To draw in different directions, distract' hence signifies 'that which causes this, a care, especially an anxious care.'"[2]

2m. To distract us from our fellowship with God.

2n. What our responsibility is and what it is not.

3a. ". . . a momentary and complete casting of one's anxiety, once for all, upon God. . . . "[3]

3b. ". . . one makes a complete surrender of himself and his all to God for Him to manage at His will. . . . "[4]

3c. ". . . reach the place where all anxiety leaves him, regardless of the outward testings that may fall to his lot."[5]

3d. The sin of independence.

3e. An immature Christian.

3f. We want to do everything for ourselves — and we end up making a terrible mess of things.

3g. Learn to cast all our care upon Him permanently.

3h. By placing ourselves totally into God's hands and allowing Him to be the Manager of our life.

3i. Our first responsibility is to trust God. The second is not to try to take His place.

4a. Our; God's; His part; "play God."

4b. God.

4c. The Holy Spirit.

4d. We are trying to do the work of the Holy Spirit.

4e. We must stop trying to play God in our own life and in the lives of other people. We must let God be God.

5a. Guidance; counsel; direction.

5b. Inform Him of what is going on; what He needs to do about it.

5c. It is our job to listen to God and let Him tell us what is going on and what we are to do about it — leaving the rest to Him to work out according to His knowledge and will, not ours.

5d. Because He is greater than we are in every aspect and area.

5e. He will teach us His ways.

6a. He is not on trial.

6b. We may be praying out of the will of God.

6c. Their inability to distinguish between God's will and personal ambition.

6d. Usually it's because what we are asking is what we want, so we assume it must be what God wants too.

6e. Some discernment.

6f. His timing. Patience and trust.

6g. Because we already have our mind made up about the way things are supposed to be, even before we go to God in prayer about them.

6h. They are really just PR sessions in which we try to manipulate God to get what we want from Him.

6i. Although we are asking, we are doing so with the wrong purpose and motives.

7a. Because we try to make things happen on our own instead of simply asking that God's will be done.

7b. Because we ask with the wrong purpose or with the wrong motives.

7c. It's because He has something better in mind for us, but we are not yet spiritually mature enough to know how to ask Him for it.

8a. She has learned not to ask Him for anything out of His will.

8b. She always prays for what she wants to have or would like to see happen, but she follows her request with this statement: "Lord, if what I am asking for is not Your will, please don't give it to me. I want Your will more than I want my own."

8c. Seek first His will and His righteousness, trusting Him to add to us all the things He knows we really need, the things that will bless us and not be a burden to us or draw us away from Him.

8d. Even if He gives them to us, having them will only cause us to sin.

8e. Spiritual life; outward blessings.

8f. God must become and always remain first in our lives.

8g. We must regularly examine our priorities and be sure they are in proper order.

8h. No, not at all. It simply means we are to trust in the Lord and put our confidence in Him.

8i. He will show us when we need to rise up against the evil spirits that come to deceive us and destroy us. If we listen to Him, we will not be so quick to start rebuking every situation that arises or every circumstance in which we find ourselves.

8j. Because sometimes what we think would be a wonderful blessing would not bless us at all.

8k. If we do, we will have to spend the rest of our days taking care of them.

8l. We need to learn to wait for God to bring forth the Isaacs in our life. They will be a blessing to us for as long as we live.

9a. Criticize, contradict, or answer back to God. We are not to ask God, "Why did You make me this way?"

9b. Potter; clay.

9c. Why He made others as they are.

9d. We are going to be unhappy.

9e. We can be used and blessed by Him as He sees fit.

9f. No. It means dishonorable in the eyes of those who do not understand God's purpose, those who think some people are more honorable and some work more important than others.

9g. We must each accept the role God has assigned us and submit ourselves to Him to mold and make us after His will and plan, and not ours.

9h. Grace is with us. Operating outside of His anointing.

9i. Now we know only in part.

9j. Trust; obey; cast our care.

10a. Our first responsibility is to trust God. Our second responsibility is to pray without worry. Our third responsibility is to avoid works of the flesh.

10b. We can be so intense we become obsessive about it, even in our prayer life.

10c. Just another work of the flesh.

10d. Being led by the Spirit.

10e. We cancel out our prayers. They become nothing more than a work of the flesh, an attempt to change things by our own energy and effort.

11a. Works.

11b. "Work" is doing by the grace of God what He has called us to do. It is the expending of our energy and effort to see the will of God come to pass in our life. But "works" is doing by our own strength and ability what we want done. It is the expending of our energy and effort to try to make happen what only God can make happen.

11c. He gives us superhuman energy.

11d. The difference between works of the flesh; the work of the Spirit.

11e. Worry, reasoning, and trying to figure out what to do to make things happen according to our will and timing.

11f. Grace.

11g. Really, truly happy.

11h. To rob us of our joy. Satan doesn't want us to be filled with contentment, peace, and rest. He wants us to be worried, confused, and upset.

11i. To take things into our own hands, as Abraham and Sarah did in the Old Testament.

12a. Abraham agreed and did as Sarah suggested.

12b. As soon as Hagar saw she was pregnant with Abraham's child, she despised Sarah and began to treat her with contempt.

12c. Sarah complained to Abraham saying, "May the responsibility for this terrible situation be upon you!"

12d. Because by agreeing with Sarah's suggestion, he failed to fulfill his God-given responsibility.

12e. Trouble and unhappiness for all concerned: Sarah, Abraham, Hagar, Ishmael, and Isaac.

12f. He was passive. Instead of truly casting his care upon the Lord and trusting Him to work out His divine plan, Abraham went along with his wife's misguided scheme.

12g. Instead of casting our care on the Lord, we cast our responsibility. We become passive, often due to laziness. It just seems to be too much trouble to take a stand on the Word of God and wait for Him to act on our behalf as we confidently trust in Him.

12h. By telling Sarah, "Well, she's your maid, do whatever you want to with her."

12i. By trying to shift it to his wife.

12j. When God questioned Adam about eating from the forbidden tree of the knowledge of good and evil, like Abraham, he tried to shift his responsibility from himself to his wife. He even went so far as to imply it was God's fault for giving Eve to him in the first place.

12k. The job of getting men to be spiritually passive and leave the responsibility for spiritual matters to the women in their lives.

12l. More and more men are beginning to seek God and become the spiritual leaders in their marriages and families.

13a. To trust God, to pray without worry, and to avoid works of the flesh.

13b. To continue in obedience during the time of waiting, to continue to bear good fruit, and to offer God a sacrifice of praise.

14a. Obedience.

14b. Make sure you are sowing seeds of obedience. Because the Lord has promised us that if we do so in patient confidence and trust in Him, we will eventually reap.

14c. God is always working. We just may not be able to see it, because He usually works in secret.

15a. Being formed in secret by the Lord.

15b. A perfect work.

15c. The Lord determined the time was right.

15d. When He knows everything is right for us.

15e. Secretly working behind the scenes. By faith.

15f. Believe He is.

15g. He is working on your behalf right now.

15h. He wants you to untie His hands.

15i. By refusing to worry and by dwelling in the secret place of the Most High, hidden away safe and secure under the shadow of His wings.

16a. Bearing good fruit.

16b. We should be like a tree planted by the water, drawing strength and life from its source because its roots go down deep into the ground. Even in times of drought, such a tree will continue to bear good fruit.

16c. We will still bear the fruit of the Spirit described in Galatians 5:22,23.

16d. Because that kind of attitude and behavior will not bring our answer.

16e. We are not to give in to them, but rather to continue to bear fruit, giving thanks and praise to God even in the midst of negative circumstances.

17a. He acknowledged God had been working secretly in his life from before his birth.

17b. For Who He is and for His wonderful works on his behalf.

17c. While we are waiting to see the fulfillment of our prayers, we are to be continually offering up to God the fruit of lips that thankfully acknowledge and confess and glorify His name.

17d. Cast our care upon the Lord, trusting Him, praying without worry, avoiding works of the flesh, continuing in obedience, bearing good fruit, and offering Him the sacrifice of praise.

Chapter 8

1a. That things will "come to pass."

1b. That in this life whatever exists now, or will exist in the future, is not permanent, but temporary.

1c. It will help us make it through the difficult times in which we find ourselves. It will also help us not to hold on too tightly to the good times, thinking, "If I ever lose all this, I just can't make it."

1d. All of life — not just its destination, but also the trip itself.

2a. (Your answers.)

2b. Moving toward some goal or objective. Another will be there.

2c. Learn to enjoy life as it unfolds.

2d. Life will pass us up and we will never enjoy where we are right now.

3a. Because they were times of preparation for the greater days the Lord knew lay ahead.

3b. Because they never get to enjoy the fruit of all their labor.

3c. Finish it.

3d. Often we are left with nobody to support us and urge us on but ourselves and God.

3e. See it through to the finish. Everything we are going through at the moment will one day pass and we will enjoy the fruit of our labor.

3f. Enjoy where we are on the way to where we are going.

4a. "This is that which was prophesied and has now come to pass."

4b. Then He moves on.

4c. We get caught up in the "This is it" mentality.

4d. Because as soon as we overcome one problem, we will have another one to overcome.

4e. Another.

4f. Prepare us for the next situation, which may be more to our liking.

4g. We can be prepared for something even better.

4h. They help us get more deeply rooted in God. They work humility in us and cause us to be very thankful when the blessings come.

4i. Training, correction, and discipline.

5. No training, correction, or discipline seems pleasant at the time it is being administered to us, "but afterwards" we come to appreciate it.

6a. 1) He will be with us, 2) He will deliver us and honor us, and 3) He will grant us long life and will show us His salvation.

6b. "No matter what you are going through at the moment, sooner or later it will pass. Someday it will all be over and done. In the meantime, cast your care upon Me and trust Me to work out everything for the best."

7a. Change us.

7b. Best friend.

7c. Things that we think are absolutely too difficult to endure.

7d. The time when the situation will be over.

7e. The fruit you are going to bear "afterwards."

7f. Realize that God is building faith in you, and "afterwards" that faith will be used to bring you into a greater realm of blessing.

7g. "This too shall pass."

8a. The forever lie and the never lie.

8b. Because sooner or later, everything changes.

8c. Bad things ultimately give way to better things.

8d. No. We might go through another hard time, but eventually through Christ, the difficulty will be changed into even better times than the ones we had previously.

8e. Then you won't be ready for the changes that surely will come.

8f. Keep our eyes on Him; make it through; growing from glory to glory.

8g. We are not to get too wrapped up in anything in this life.

8h. To the Lord alone and not to anyone or anything else.

8i. Think we could not live without it.

8j. "Get detached from your attachments."

8k. Stewards; owners.

8l. We must always be free to move with the Spirit.

8m. Let it go.

8n. We try to hang on to the past, when God is saying, "It's time to move on to something new."

8o. Let it go. Look to the new thing and allow it to "come to pass." Don't live in the past when God has a new season for you. Let go of what lies behind and press on to what lies ahead.

8p. Reach out toward that new horizon God has for you. That's what Abraham did — and God blessed him for it.

9a. To leave his country, his home, and his relatives and go to a place He would show him.

9b. It had "come to pass," and it was time for her to move on to something else.

9c. No, it just means God was finished with that season in her life.

9d. Do what He wants to do in each of those seasons.

9e. Because everything is changing all the time, and so must we.

9f. "This too shall pass."

9g. God and His will and plan for us.

10a. Because if our outer man has things broken off, the powerful things inside us can pour forth.

10b. The alabaster box, which is the flesh, has to be broken.

10c. We must allow God to deal with us and do with us as He wills. We must learn to lean on Him and trust in Him completely, knowing that everything in life changes.

10d. This was done to keep him from becoming too proud by reminding him, "This too shall pass."

10e. He gives us His Holy Spirit to fill us and empower us and use us as a blessing to others. But He also sends His Holy Spirit to remind us that "this too shall pass."

10f. We must quit looking for one thing that will be "it." We must recall that life is a continual process in which everything is constantly changing — including us.

10g. He is the only thing in this world Who does not change. He is the same yesterday, today, and forever.

11a. Maturity.

11b. To come to the place that we can be content no matter what our situation or circumstances may be, because we are rooted and grounded, not in things, but in the Lord.

11c. Because he knew whatever state he may be in at the moment, it too would pass.

11d. He said he had learned the secret of facing every situation of life, whether good or bad.

11e. We would soon become soft and spoiled. We would assume anybody who was not being blessed as much as we were was doing something wrong. We would try to give that individual "victory lessons."

11f. Spiritual pride.

11g. How to handle new realms of blessings without developing a wrong attitude.

11h. God allows that to happen occasionally so we will learn to keep things in perspective.

11i. We get spoiled and prideful.

11j. We become discouraged and despondent.

11k. "This too shall pass."

11l. Nothing — good or bad — lasts forever.

12a. Walked through.

12b. We are just passing through. Whatever may be happening to us at the moment, in time it too shall pass.

12c. How fast things can change.

12d. "Wrong! Things may be this way right now, but whether they change or not makes no difference to me — I'm just passing through!"

12e. "When you pass through the waters, I will be with you, and through the rivers, they will not overwhelm you. When you walk through the fire, you will not be burned or scorched, nor will the flame kindle upon you."

12f. Because they trusted themselves to the Lord, they didn't stay there to be consumed by the flames. They came through them to victory.

12g. Daniel came through that experience unharmed.

12h. The same kind of protection and deliverance to all those who put their faith and trust in Him.

13a. That we will never change.

13b. That as we behold the glory of God we ". . . are changed into the same image from glory to glory, even as by the Spirit of the Lord."

13c. A complete change from one thing to something totally different, as when a caterpillar enters a cocoon as a worm and later emerges as a butterfly.[3]

13d. It is the kind of process we are going through spiritually, as we change from the old man to the new man.

13e. "No, I'm not. I'm in the process of change. I won't be a worm forever, you just wait and see. One day I'll be something totally different from what I am right now. I'll be a beautiful butterfly!"

13f. We would never develop the strength and stamina we need to survive in this world.

13g. "Suddenlies."

14a. A "season of suddenlies."

14b. "In a moment, in the twinkling of an eye" — in other words, suddenly.

14c. Because no matter what remains to be done in the transformation of our old man into our new man, it will be accomplished suddenly — at the appearing of Jesus in the heavenlies.

14d. Changing us from glory to glory; remains to be changed in us; suddenly.

14e. Just as suddenly.

14f. Supernaturally; ordinarily; suddenly; over a period of time.

14g. How Jesus appeared to Paul and changed him from a persecutor of the Church to a brand-new convert who would later become the leading apostle to the Gentiles.

14h. If God could suddenly confront and change Paul, He can confront and change anybody.

14i. Because sometimes God works suddenly, and sometimes He works over a period of time.

14j. He works in response to prayer and praise.

14k. In a supernatural way or in an ordinary way. But He is moving on your behalf.

14l. Cast it all on the Lord so you can retire from care.

Chapter 9

1a. Giving ourselves up to God, taking ourselves out of our own keeping, and entrusting ourselves into His keeping.

1b. Self-care.

1c. Basically, it stems from the idea that if we do it, we can be sure it will be done right. We are afraid of what might happen if we entrust ourselves totally to God and He doesn't "come through" for us.

1d. Trusting ourselves more than we trust God.

1e. God has a plan for us too — and His plan is much better than ours.

2a. God wants to help us, but He wants to do it His way and not our way — because our way usually involves a lot of worry, fretfulness, reasoning, anxiety, and excessive plotting and planning.

2b. To hear God's plan.

2c. Become so rooted and grounded in our plan that we argue and resist if God tries to show us a better way.

2d. That she would never enjoy her life until she began trusting God to a much greater degree.

2e. Because He knows that apart from Him we can do nothing.

2f. In everything that concerns us, God has a plan, just as He did for Jesus when He sent Him into this world to save us and to serve as our example.

3a. Consulted God. The will of His Father. It was not His decision. It was the will of the One Who Sent Him.

3b. He was not independent, out on His own trying to do His own thing.

3c. We figure out what we want and ask God to bless it.

3d. To do the will and pleasure of His heavenly Father.

3e. "What you see Me doing is what I see the Father doing. What you hear Me saying is what I hear the Father saying. I do not speak on My own authority, but on His authority."

3f. We should realize that anything we do independently, apart from God, will fail to bear any good fruit either for Him or for us.

4a. Knows what will truly bless us and make us happy and orders our steps to bring us into what He has for us.

4b. They plan everything according to what they think is the best plan for them.

4c. To seek God's will and plan for our life rather than our own.

4d. Go off independently on our own trying to fulfill our own desires or meet our own needs.

4e. Trust in the Lord with all our heart and mind, and not lean on our own understanding.

5a. No, that would not be possible.

5b. God puts wisdom into us in the form of His Holy Spirit, for us to walk by that wisdom step-by-step.

5c. Know, recognize, and acknowledge. His Spirit; quiet confidence, trust, and obedience.

5d. To be aware of and care about what we are doing.

5e. Because He will direct our paths.

5f. He will nudge us and get us back on the right path.

5g. Insulting; consulting; what we want.

5h. It displays a lack of trust in God.

5i. Because we don't want to become dependent upon anyone.

5j. So we will have to work together to accomplish His will in our lives.

5k. Get involved with other people.

5l. So we have no choice but to lean on Him and on others.

5m. He acknowledged that he and his people had no might to stand against such a great company, adding, "We don't know what to do, Lord, but our eyes are on You."

5n. That is the statement of a person who is dependent on God, not independent.

6a. Anointing.

6b. So that all the glory will go to Him and not to them.

6c. God either calls people with talent then spends years teaching them that without His anointing their talents will do them absolutely no good, or He calls people who are so incapable they know the only way they can ever hope to do anything is by leaning totally on Him every second.

6d. The first disciples Jesus called.

6e. That they were all losers and that He would get nowhere with them because they would never be of any value to Him.

6f. So He can use them to confound the wise and powerful.

6g. Zeros; power; great for His glory.

6h. Because if we do we will fail every time.

6i. Recognize and acknowledge our utter dependence on God.

6j. We have learned through bitter experience nobody in this world is going to look out for us or have our best interests at heart but us.

6k. Keeping total control over every aspect of your life.

6l. Almost impossible to do so.

6m. Your refusal to cast your care upon the Lord and entrust yourself to His keeping.

7a. Upon those rebellious children who turn from trusting in Him to take counsel of themselves, carry out their own plans, and flee to "the shadow of Egypt" rather than resting under the "shadow of the Almighty."

7b. Turning to the arm of the flesh rather than leaning on the arm of the Lord.

7c. The Lord.

7d. Acknowledge the Lord in all our ways so that He may direct our paths.

7e. Him; ourselves; the world.

8a. "Don't turn away from trusting in Me to trusting in your own plans and devices. They won't work, and you will only end up humiliated and confused."

8b. "Before you do anything, check with Me to see if it is what you should be doing. Don't look to the world for answers, because it has none to give. Salvation and deliverance are with Me, and Me alone."

9a.   We leave a weak spot in our wall of divine protection.

9b.   The enemy will break through that weak spot.

9c.   He wants us to rely on Him and be obedient to Him so our wall will remain strong and thick and our lives will be blessed and full.

9d.   He can do through us. Brokenness; blessings.

9e.   Remind us of our place.

9f.   The solution to our problems is found in Him and Him alone.

10a. "Either you are going to depend on Me, or you are going to end up in the biggest mess you have ever seen in your whole life."

10b. If we don't, we will not be able to do anything of any value. Apart from Him we can do nothing.

11a. That he had run his own life for a long time — often walking according to emotions and his own will — but now it was time to grow up. It was time to turn the reins of his life over to God.

11b. That he might not like everything that was going to happen, but that it would ultimately end up for the glory of God.

11c. He blessed our plans and let them work.

11d. God no longer blesses and prospers our childish plans and schemes.

11e. He has begun establishing His way in our individual lives.

11f. To put our trust in Him and not in ourselves.

11g. He knew Peter's love was about to be put to the test.

11h. No, He is just asking us to lay it on the altar, as Abraham lay Isaac on the altar before the Lord.

11i. Because we must not let anything — even our work for God — become more important to us than God Himself.

11j. By asking us to lay down our most treasured blessing as proof of our love for Him.

11k. He will begin to honor us and work out His plan for our life.

11l. Because of his tendency to give into the flesh.

11m. He told Peter He was praying for him — just as He is praying for us right now.

12a. Peter's faith would not fail him while he was going through that time of testing.

12b. He is praying we will come through the times of testing in our lives and emerge from them strengthened and empowered so that we can strengthen and empower others to live in joy, peace, and victory.

12c. Face the enemy.

12d. He may not always do everything exactly as we would like it done or just when we would like it to be done. But whatever He does do will be right, the thing that is best in that situation.

13a. "I am sending you out to do a job for Me, but don't take anything with you to take care of yourselves."

13b. The point is not that we are forbidden to take pocketbooks and shoes and clothes with us when we travel from one place to another to minister. The point is that we are to be obedient to do the will of God, trusting Him to meet the needs He knows we will experience.

13c. Make the arrangements necessary to keep us provisioned.

13d. If we will tend to His harvest, He will tend to our needs.

14a. They didn't go out seeking gifts.

14b. Because they were in the middle of God's will, He sent them Wise Men from the east mounted on camels loaded down with provisions.

14c. If we are in the will of God, He will always bring our provision to us. We don't have to chase it down; it will seek us out. We don't have to try to make things happen; God will bring them to us.

14d. We need to back off and consult the Lord. That may not be the way God wants us to go.

14e. So we will be open to follow another.

14f. Just keep confessing, "The camels are coming!" And eventually they will arrive — on God's schedule, not ours.

14g. Stay in the will of God.

14h. Being faithful to stay where God has placed us and do the work He has given us to do for His Kingdom's sake.

14i. We are free to cast our care upon Him. We don't have to stay up all night fretting and worrying, trying to figure out what to do to take care of ourselves. We can simply deposit ourselves with God.

15a. Deposit ourselves with God, trusting Him to take care of us.

15b. When we are being ill-treated and are suffering because we belong to God and are doing right, being faithful to His will for us.

15c. We must quit trying to seek justice for ourselves and simply trust Him to justify us and work out everything for the best in accordance with His will and plan. That's what Jesus did.

15d. Jesus did not respond in kind. Instead, He trusted Himself entirely to God Who judges all things and all people fairly and justly.

15e.	Like Him, we are not to try to take matters into our own hands, but instead to commit ourselves to God, trusting Him to work out everything for good to all concerned.

15f.	We spend so much time trying to take care of ourselves. We are too busy with self-care, trying to make sure that nobody takes advantage of us, that everyone treats us right, that we get our fair share.

15g.	We will fail to do what we are called to do, which is to minister to the needs of others.

15h.	We must continue to do the work God has set before us. We must deposit ourselves with Him, trusting Him to justify us and vindicate us, to protect us and provide for us, to help us and keep us.

16a.	A beautiful hymn about God as the Helper and Keeper of those who trust in Him.

16b.	Read and meditate on it constantly.

16c.	By the eyelid. The moment danger threatens, the eyelid automatically closes, shutting out anything harmful. That is what God does for us who entrust ourselves to Him.

17a.	". . . He is the rewarder of those who earnestly and diligently seek Him [out]."

17b.	Rewards; recompenses.

17c.	A back pay, sort of like Workers' Compensation.

18a.	He means that sooner or later He will make everything right. He will see we get everything coming to us.

18b.	Pray for our enemies, for those who mistreat us, abuse us, and take advantage of us.

18c.	To take care of us.

18d.	He determines and solves and settles the cause and the cases of His people.

18e.	With Jesus as our Friend, the Holy Spirit as our Advocate, and the heavenly Father as our Judge, we can retire from self-care, knowing that justice will be done — so that we can be anxious for nothing.

Endnotes

Introduction

[1] Romans 8:28.

Chapter 2

[1] *Webster's II New Riverside Desk Dictionary* (Boston: Houghton Mifflin Company, 1988), s.v. "anxiety."

[2] *Webster's New World College Dictionary*, 3rd ed. (New York: Macmillan, 1996), s.v. "anxiety."

Chapter 6

[1] James E. Strong, "Hebrew and Chaldee Dictionary," in *Strong's Exhaustive Concordance of the Bible* (Nashville: Abingdon, 1890), p. 52, entry #3427, s.v. "dwell," Psalm 91:1.

Chapter 7

[1] Based on definitions from W.E. Vine, Merrill F. Unger, William White Jr., *Vine's Complete Expository Dictionary of Old and New Testament Words* (Nashville: Thomas Nelson, Inc., 1984), "New Testament Section," p. 91, s.v. "CAST," A. Verbs.

[2] Vine, p. 89, s.v. "CARE (noun and verb), CAREFUL, CAREFULLY, CAREFULNESS," A. Nouns, 1.

[3] Footnote to 1 Peter 5:8 written by A.S. Worrell in *The Worrell New Testament* (Springfield, MO: Gospel Publishing House, 1980), p. 352.

[4] Footnote to 1 Peter 5:8 written by A.S. Worrell in *The Worrell New Testament* (Springfield, MO: Gospel Publishing House, 1980), p. 352.

[5] Footnote to 1 Peter 5:8 written by A.S. Worrell in *The Worrell New Testament* (Springfield, MO: Gospel Publishing House, 1980), p. 352.

Chapter 8

[1] Tingay and Badcock, *These Were the Romans* (Chester Springs, PA: Dufour Editions, Inc., 1989).

[2] James E. Strong, "Greek Dictionary of the New Testament," in *Strong's Exhaustive Concordance of the Bible* (Nashville: Abingdon, 1890), p. 47, entry #3339, s.v. "change," 2 Corinthians 3:18.

[3] Based on definition in Webster's 3d, s.v. "metamorphosis": "a marked or complete change of character, appearance, condition, etc."; "the physical transformation, more or less sudden, undergone by various animals during development after the embryonic state. . . ."

About the Author

Joyce Meyer has been teaching the Word of God since 1976 and in full-time ministry since 1980. Previously the associate pastor at Life Christian Center in St. Louis, Missouri, she developed, coordinated, and taught a weekly meeting known as "Life In The Word." After more than five years, the Lord brought it to a conclusion, directing her to establish her own ministry and call it *"Life In The Word, Inc."*

Now, her *Life In The Word* radio and television broadcasts are seen and heard by millions across the United States and throughout the world. Joyce's teaching tapes are enjoyed internationally, and she travels extensively conducting *Life In The Word* conferences.

Joyce and her husband, Dave, the business administrator at *Life In The Word,* have been married for over 34 years. They reside in St. Louis, Missouri, and are the parents of four children. All four children are married and, along with their spouses, work with Dave and Joyce in the ministry.

Believing the call on her life is to establish believers in God's Word, Joyce says, "Jesus died to set the captives free, and far too many Christians have little or no victory in their daily lives." Finding herself in the same situation many years ago and having found freedom to live in victory through applying God's Word, Joyce goes equipped to set captives free and to exchange ashes for beauty. She believes that every person who walks in victory leads many others into victory. Her life is transparent, and her teachings are practical and can be applied in everyday life.

Joyce has taught on emotional healing and related subjects in meetings all over the country, helping multiplied thousands. She has recorded more than 225 different audiocassette albums and over 70 videos. She has also authored 47 books to help the body of Christ on various topics.

Her "Emotional Healing Package" contains over 23 hours of teaching on the subject. Albums included in this package are: "Confidence"; "Beauty for

Ashes" (includes a syllabus — Joyce's teaching notes); "Managing Your Emotions"; "Bitterness, Resentment, and Unforgiveness"; "Root of Rejection"; and a 90-minute Scripture/music tape titled "Healing the Brokenhearted."

Joyce's "Mind Package" features five different audio tape series on the subject of the mind. They include: "Mental Strongholds and Mindsets"; "Wilderness Mentality"; "The Mind of the Flesh"; "The Wandering, Wondering Mind"; and "Mind, Mouth, Moods, and Attitudes." The package also contains Joyce's powerful book, *Battlefield of the Mind.* On the subject of love she has three tape series titled "Love Is..."; "Love: The Ultimate Power"; and "Loving God, Loving Yourself, and Loving Others," and a book titled *Reduce Me to Love.*

Write to Joyce Meyer's office for a resource catalog and further information on how to obtain the tapes you need to bring total healing to your life.

To contact the author write:
Joyce Meyer Ministries
P. O. Box 655 • Fenton, Missouri 63026
or call: (636) 349-0303
Internet Address: www.joycemeyer.org

Please include your testimony or help received from this book when you write. Your prayer requests are welcome.

To contact the author in Canada, please write:
Joyce Meyer Ministries Canada, Inc.
Lambeth Box 1300 • London, ON N6P 1T5
or call: (636) 349-0303

In Australia, please write:
Joyce Meyer Ministries-Australia
Locked Bag 77 • Mansfield Delivery Centre
Queensland 4122 • or call: (07) 3349 1200

In England, please write:
Joyce Meyer Ministries
P. O. Box 1549 • Windsor • SL4 1GT
or call: 01753 831102

Books by Joyce Meyer

Filled with the Spirit

A Celebration of Simplicity

The Joy of Believing Prayer

Never Lose Heart

Being the Person God Made You to Be

A Leader in the Making

"Good Morning, This Is God!" Gift Book

JESUS — Name Above All Names

"Good Morning, This Is God!" Daily Calendar

Help Me — I'm Married!

Reduce Me to Love

Be Healed in Jesus' Name

How to Succeed at Being Yourself

Eat and Stay Thin

Weary Warriors, Fainting Saints

Life in the Word Journal

Life in the Word Devotional

Be Anxious for Nothing

NEW: *Be Anxious for Nothing Study Guide*

The Help Me! Series:
I'm Alone!
I'm Stressed! • I'm Insecure!
I'm Discouraged! • I'm Depressed!
I'm Worried! • I'm Afraid!

Don't Dread

Managing Your Emotions

Healing the Brokenhearted

"Me and My Big Mouth!"

"Me and My Big Mouth!" Study Guide

Prepare to Prosper

Do It! Afraid

*Expect a Move of God in Your Life...**Suddenly***

Enjoying Where You Are on the Way to Where You Are Going

The Most Important Decision You'll Ever Make

When, God, When?

Why, God, Why?

The Word, the Name, the Blood

Battlefield of the Mind

Battlefield of the Mind Study Guide

Tell Them I Love Them

Peace

The Root of Rejection

Beauty for Ashes

If Not for the Grace of God

By Dave Meyer

Nuggets of Life

Available from your local bookstore.